The Word and Art

The Word and Art

Poetic Reflections on Art 1300–2024

STEPHEN FALCONER

RESOURCE *Publications* • Eugene, Oregon

THE WORD AND ART
Poetic Reflections on Art 1300–2024

Copyright © 2025 Stephen Falconer. All rights reserved. Except for brief quotations in critical publications or reviews, no part of this book may be reproduced in any manner without prior written permission from the publisher. Write: Permissions, Wipf and Stock Publishers, 199 W. 8th Ave., Suite 3, Eugene, OR 97401.

Resource Publications
An Imprint of Wipf and Stock Publishers
199 W. 8th Ave., Suite 3
Eugene, OR 97401

www.wipfandstock.com

PAPERBACK ISBN: 979-8-3852-4458-4
HARDCOVER ISBN: 979-8-3852-4459-1
EBOOK ISBN: 979-8-3852-4460-7

VERSION NUMBER 04/22/25

Contents

14th Century

John the Baptist, *Byzantine Icon*	3
Pietà Röttgen, *German Sculpture*	5
Golden Buddha of Sukhothai	6
Transfiguration, *Duccio*	7
The Dormition of the Virgin Mary, *Giotto*	8
St Geminianus, *Simone Martini*	10
The Great East Window, *Gloucester Cathedral*	12
The Marriage of the Virgin, *Niccolo di Bonaccorso*	14
Wilton Diptych	16

15th Century

Bird in Plum Tree, *Kano Kakusho*	19
Dish with Design of Pine Trees, *Blue and White Jingdezhen Ware*	20
Madonna and Child with St Anne, *Masaccio/Masolino*	22
Expulsion from the Garden of Eden, *Masaccio*	23
Mary Magdalene's Sea Voyage to France, *Lucas Moser*	24
The Journey of the Magi, *Sassetta*	26
Arnolfini Portrait, *Jan van Eyck*	28
Portrait of a Woman with a Winged Bonnet, *Rogier van der Weyden*	30

Contents

The Baptism of Christ, *Piero della Francesca*	32
The Vision of Saint Eustace, *Pisanello*	34
Saint Lawrence Enthroned with Saints Cosmos, and Damian and Demos *Fra Filippo Lippi*	36
David, *Donatello*	38
The Annunciation, *Fra Angelico*	40
Landscape, *Dai Jin*	42
John the Baptist, *Antonio Vivarini*	44
Agony in the Gardens, *Andrea Mantegna*	45
Saint Sebastian, *Andrea Mantegna*	47
Portrait of a Young Woman, *Antonio or Piero del Pollaiuolo*	48
Hunt in the Forest, *Paolo Uccello*	50
St Jerome in his Study, *Antonello da Messina*	52
Dama del Mazzolino, *Andrea del Verrocchio*	54
Portrait of a Young Man, *Domenico Ghirlandaio*	55
Sultan Mehmet II Smelling a Rose, *Ottoman*	57
The Birth of Venus, *Sandro Botticelli*	59
The Annunciation, with Saint Emidius, *Carlo Crivelli*	60
St. Augustine, *Carlo Crivelli*	61
Autumn Landscape, *Sesshu*	63

16th Century

Taking a Lute to Visit a Friend, *Jiang Song*	67
The Peddler, *Hieronymus Bosch*	68
The Entombment, *Michaelangelo*	69
Self Portrait, *Albrecht Durer*	70
Samson and Delilah, *Andrea Mantegna*	72
Doge Leonardo Loredan, *Giovanni Bellini*	73
Mona Lisa, *Leonardo Da Vinci*	75
Piper and Drummer, *Albrecht Dürer*	77
The Ansidei Madonna, *Raphael*	78

Contents

Pope Julius II, *Raphael*	80
The Temptation of Saint Anthony, *Matthias Grünewald*	82
Dying Slave, *Michelangelo*	83
Belem Madonna and Child (Our Lady of the Grapes)	84
Christ Showing His Wounds, *German Sculpture*	86
The Crucifixion of Christ, *Matthias Grünewald*	88
Assumption of the Virgin, *Titian*	89
Resurrection, *Matthias Grünewald*	91
Landscape with a Footbridge, *Albrecht Altdorfer*	92
An Allegory on the Sack of Rome, *Francesco Xanto Avelli*	94
Portrait of the Merchant Georg Giese, *Hans Holbein the Younger*	95
Ecce Homo, *Titian*	97
Wintry Trees, *Wen Zhengming*	98
Cosimo 1 de 'Medici in Armor, *Agnolo Bronzino*	99
Portrait of a Young Man as David, *Tintoretto*	100
Great Rockery, *Pan Yunduan*	101
Samson Slaying Philistines, *Giovanni Bologna*	102
Harvesters, *Pieter Bruegel the Elder*	103
Nobleman between Active and Contemplative, *Life Paolo Veronese*	105
Abduction of a Sabine Woman, *Giambologna*	107
Venus and Adonis, *Bartholomeus Spranger*	108

17th Century

Christ driving the Traders from the Temple, *El Greco*	113
Christ Appearing to St Peter on the Appian Way *Annibale Carracci*	115
Winter Landscape with Bird Trap, *Pieter Breughel the Younger*	117
The Supper at Emmaus, *Caravaggio*	119
David with the Head of Goliath, *Caravaggio*	120

Contents

Black-capped Kingfisher, *Mughal*	122
Elevation of the Cross, *Rubens*	123
Qur'an Commissioned by Sultan 'Abdullah II Al Sa'adi	125
The Watering Place, *Rubens*	126
Neptune and Triton, *Gian Lorenzo Bernini*	127
Aesop, *Jusepe de Ribera*	128
Two Old Men Disputing, *Rembrandt*	129
Yasoda Nursing the Child Krishna, *Bhagavata Purana Manuscript*	131
The Crossing of the Red Sea, *Nicolas Poussin*	133
Diego Felipe de Guzman, Marquis of Leganes, *Anthony van Dyck*	135
Saint Francis in Meditation, *Francisco de Zurbaran*	137
Lucretia, *Guido Reni*	138
Dune Landscape by Moonlight, *Adriaen Brower*	139
Harbor Scene with Lamenting Heliades, *Claude Lorraine*	141
Venus and Adonis, *Francesco Fanelli*	142
Night watch, *Rembrandt*	144
Italian Landscape, *Jan Both*	146
Confirmation, *Nicolas Poussin*	148
Toilet of Venus, *Diego Velazquez*	149
Pastoral with the Arch of Constantine, *Claude Lorraine*	151
The Embarkation of the Queen of Sheba, *Claude Lorraine*	153
View of La Crescenza, *Claude Lorraine*	155
A Man in Armor, *Rembrandt*	156
Franciscan Friar, *Rembrandt*	158
Wooded Hillside with a View of Bentheim Castle, *Jacob van Ruisdael*	159
A Lady with a Pink, *Rembrandt*	161
Winter (The Flood), *Nicolas Poussin*	162
Woman with a Pearl Necklace, *Johannes Vermeer*	164
Self Portrait 63 years, *Rembrandt*	166

Contents

Charles II, *John Bushnell*	167
Ascanius Shooting the Stag of Sylvia, *Claude Lorraine*	169
Landscape in the Style of Huang Gongwang, *Wang Yanqui*	171
The Avenue at Middelharnis, *Meindert Hobbema*	172
Buddha, *Tennoji Temple*	173

18th Century

White Magnolia, Hemp Palm and Banana Plants, *Tatebayashi Kagei*	177
Venus Disarming Cupid, *Corneille van Cleve*	178
Irises, *Ogata Korin*	180
Francois Armand di Goutant, *Nicolas de largilliere*	182
The Dance, *Antoine Watteau*	184
Penglai, Island of the Immortals, *Yuan Jiang*	186
Flowers in a Vase, *Jan van Huysum*	187
Sleeping Shepherdess, *Nicolas Lancret*	188
The School Mistress, *Jean Simeon Chardin*	189
Handel, *Louis-Francois Roubiliac*	191
The Piazza San Marco, *Canaletto*	193
The Banquet of Cleopatra, *Giambattista Tiepolo*	195
The Painter and his Pug, *William Hogarth*	196
The Mysterious Basket, *Francois Boucher*	197
Portrait of an Old Woman, *Christian Seybold*	199
Portrait Group: The Singer Farinelli and Friends, *Jacopo Amigoni*	200
Poetess Ono no Komachi, *Harunobu*	201
Self Portrait, *Marie-Gabrielle Capet*	202
Landscape with Shepherds and Flock of Sheep, *Jean-Honore Fragonard*	203
Miss Susannah Gale, *Sir Joshua Reynolds*	204
Floating Angel, *Ignaz Gunther*	206
Seaport by Moonlight, *Joseph Vernet*	207

Contents

View of the Venetian Lagoon with the Tower of Malghera, *Francesco Guardi*	208
The House of Cards, *Jean-Simeon Chardin*	210
Diana and her Nymphs Bathing, *Angelica Kauffman*	212
The Listening Girl, *Jean-Baptiste Greuze*	214
Self Portrait in a Straw Hat, *Élisabeth Loise Vigée Le Brun*	215
The Death of Major Pierson, *John Singleton Copley*	216
Theodore Meets in the Wood the Specter of His Ancestor Guido Cavalcanti, *Johann Fuseli*	217
Mr and Mrs William Hallett ('The Morning Walk'), *Thomas Gainsborough*	219
The Death of Socrates, *Jacques-Louis David*	221
Italian Landscape with Bathers, *Pierre Henri de Valenciennes*	223
The Lovers, Chubei and Umegawa, *Kitagawa Utamaro*	224
A Scene from 'The Forcibly Bewitched', *Francisco de Goya*	226

19th Century

Napoleon as Mars the Peacemaker, *Antonio Canova*	231
Theseus and the Centaur, *Antonio Canova*	232
William Blake, *Thomas Phillips*	233
Goethe, *Gerhard von Kügelen*	235
Winter Landscape, *Caspar David Friedrich*	236
Truth Has Died, *Francisco Goya*	238
The Mutiny on the Raft of the Medusa, *Théodore Géricault*	240
Meditating Frog, *Sengai Gibon*	242
Hay Wain, *John Constable*	243
Salisbury Cathedral from the Bishop's Grounds, *John Constable*	245
Old Beech Tree, *Camille Corot*	246
Great Wave off the Coast of Kanagawa, *Katsushika Hokusai*	248
Landscape with a Clump of Trees, *Théodore Rousseau*	250
Rain, Steam and Speed, *William Turner*	252

Contents

Mongolian Invasion, *Kikushi Yosai*	254
Boston Harbor, *Fitz Henry Lane*	255
Romans of the Decadence, *Anselm Feuerbach*	256
Ophelia, *John Millais*	258
Paysage Huile Sur Toile, *Gustave Courbet*	260
End of the Hamlet of Gruchy, *Jean-Francois Millet*	261
Madame Moitessier, *Jean Auguste Dominique Ingres*	263
The Neapolitan Fisher boy, *Jean-Baptiste Carpeaux*	265
Angelica and the Wounded Medoro, *Eugène Delacroix*	266
Oedipus and the Sphynx, *Gustave Moreau*	268
Paolo and Francesca da Rimini, *Dante Gabriel Rossetti*	270
The Walk, *Paul Cézanne*	272
Nocturne: Blue and Silver-Chelsea, *James Abbott Mc Neill Whistler*	273
Lake Nemi, *George Innes*	275
The Trout, *Gustave Courbet*	277
Salome at the Prison, *Gustave Moreau*	278
Snow at Louveciennes, *Alfred Sisley*	279
Going to Evening Church, *Samuel Palmer*	280
Portrait of Renee Delmas de Pont-Jest, *Louise Abbema*	282
Woman in Black, *Berthe Morisot*	284
Côte des Boeufs at L'Hermitage, *Camille Pissarro*	286
Jews Praying in the Synagogue at Yom Kippur, *Maurycy Gottlieb*	288
Island of the Dead, *Arnold Böcklin*	290
The Tea, *Mary Cassatt*	291
Three Dancers in the Wings, *Edgar Degas*	293
The Cliff at Fécamp, *Claude Monet*	295
Luncheon of the Boating Party, *Pierre-Auguste Renoir*	296
The Thinker, *Auguste Rodin*	298
A Bar at the Folies-Bergère, *Edouard Manet*	300
Bathers at Asnières, *Georges Seurat*	302

Contents

Cooling Off at Shijo, *Yoshitoshi Tsukioka*	304
Moon at the Pleasure Quarters, *Yoshitoshi Tsukioka*	305
View from Montmartre, *Vincent Van Gogh*	306
The Montagne Sainte-Victoire with a Large Pine, *Paul Cézanne*	307
Self Portrait before Easel, *Vincent Van Gogh*	309
Ravine, *Vincent Van Gogh*	310
Field of Poppies near Giverny, *Claude Monet*	311
Near Heidelberg, *Arthur Streeton*	312
The Road to Copenhagen from Kastrup, *Theodor Philipsen*	314
The Streetwalker, *Henri Toulouse Lautrec*	316
Young Girl with a Hen, *Maurice Denis*	317
Crouching Woman, *Auguste Rodin*	319
Sheep in a Snowstorm, *Joseph Farquharson*	320
In a Corner on the Macintyre, *Tom Roberts*	321
Nevermore, *Paul Gaugin*	323
The Boulevard Montmartre at Night, *Camille Pissarro*	325
Chrysanthemums, *Claude Monet*	327
Pan Reading to a Woman by a Brook, *Aubrey Beardsley*	329

20th Century

Notre Dame, *Henri Matisse*	333
Summit of the King William Range, *William Piguenit*	335
Chateau Noir, *Paul Cézanne*	337
Pegasus, *Odilon Redon*	339
The Blind Man's Meal, *Pablo Picasso*	341
Sailing Boats at Chatou, *Maurice de Vlaminck*	343
The Pool of London, *André Derain*	345
L'Eau ou La Baigneuse, *Frantisek Kupka*	347
Hope, II, *Gustav Klimt*	349
Les Demoiselles D'Avignon, *Pablo Picasso*	350

Contents

The Doge's Palace Seen from San Giorgio Maggiore, *Claude Monet*	352
Houses at L'Estaque, *Georges Braque*	354
Streetlight, *Giacomo Balla*	356
Workers in the Snow, *Edvard Munch*	357
Glass of Absinthe, *Georges Braque*	359
I and the Village, *Marc Chagall*	361
Indian Totem Pole, *Emily Carr*	363
Street, Berlin, *Ernst Ludwig Kirchner*	365
Bowl of Fruit, Violin and Bottle, *Pablo Picasso*	367
Workshop, *Wyndham Lewis*	369
Woman Combing Her Hair, *Alexander Archipenko*	370
Water Lillies, *Claude Monet*	372
Anna Zborowska, *Amedeo Modigliani*	373
Fountain, *Marcel Duchamp*	375
Syphon, Glass and Newspaper, *Juan Gris*	377
Metaphysical Muses (Masks), *Giorgio de Chirico*	379
M'Amenez-y, *Francis Picabia*	381
Around a Point, *Frantisek Kupka*	382
Still Life, *Amédée Ozenfant*	384
Comedy, *Paul Klee*	385
Man in a Green Coat, *Chaim Soutine*	386
Nude with Drapery, *Suzanne Valadon*	387
Vernnonet, *Pierre Bonnard*	389
Composition with Blue, Red, Yellow and Black, *Piet Mondrian*	390
The Representation of Humanity, *Rudolf Steiner*	391
Pieta or Revolution by Night, *Max Ernst*	393
The Mandrill, *Oskar Kokoschka*	395
Boats and Cliffs, *Paul Klee*	396
October Morning, *Clarice Beckett*	398
The Curve of the Bridge, *Grace Cossington Smith*	399

Contents

Circular Forms, *Robert Delaunay*	401
The Persistence of Memory, *Salvador Dali*	403
Towers over City Hall, *Lyonel Feininger*	405
Voice of Space, *René Magritte*	406
Ad Parnassum, *Paul Klee*	408
Dining Room on the Garden, *Pierre Bonnard*	410
Hirosaki Castle, *Yoshida Hiroshi*	412
Yellow Middle, *Wassily Kandinsky*	414
Crown of Buds II, *Hans Arp*	416
Weeping Woman, *Pablo Picasso*	418
Death and Fire, *Paul Klee*	419
Good Hope Road, *Ashile Gorky*	421
First-class Marksman, *Sidney Nolan*	423
A Man Pointing, *Alberto Giacometti*	424
Eidos, *Barbara Hepworth*	425
Interior with Egyptian Curtain, *Henri Matisse*	427
Autumn Rhythm, *Jackson Pollock*	429
Vir Heroicus Sublimus, *Barnet Newman*	431
Christ of St John of the Cross, *Salvador Dali*	432
Italian Square, *Giorgio de Chirico*	433
The Blue Phantom, *Wols*	434
The Invisibles, *Yves Tanguy*	436
Kerrhon, *Victor Vasarely*	438
Red Cock and Blue Sky, *Fernand Léger*	440
Collins St, 5 p.m., *John Brack*	442
The Jostlers, *Jeffrey Smart*	443
Opening, *Bridget Riley*	445
Campbell Soup Cans, *Andy Warhol*	446
Untitled, *Mark Rothko*	447
Maimonides, *Amadeo Olmos Ruiz*	448
Message from a Friend, *Joan Miro*	449
Girl with Hair Ribbon, *Roy Lichtenstein*	450

Contents

A Bigger Splash, *David Hockney*	452
The Ancestral Guwark, *Narritjin Maymuru*	454
Khurasan Gate Variation II, *Frank Stella*	455
Mausoleum of Mohammed V, *Cong Vo Toan*	456
Distorted Circle within Polygon II, *Robert Mangold*	458
Merlion	459
Columnade, *Eduardo Ramirez Villamizar*	460
Solstice, *Lesley Dumbrell*	461
Study for Self Portrait, *Francis Bacon*	463
Dove, *Éric de Saussure*	464
Changes and Disappearances, *John Cage*	466
He Came Bringing Tallow, *Joseph Beuys*	467
Mother and Child, *Henry Moore*	469
Mountains, *Miriam Cahn*	470
Suspended Stone Circle II, *Ken Unsworth*	471
The Dance, *Paula Rego*	473
Two Lakes in Virgin Forest, *Kyuichiro Aihara*	475
Look at an Apple, Digest an Image, A Self-portrait, *Remy Zaugg*	476
Goddess, *Jangarh Singh Shyam*	477
Iron: Man, *Antony Gormley*	479
Untitled from Flight Fantasy series, *David Hammons*	480
Mamam, *Louise Bourgeois*	482
Wanjina, *Lily Karadada*	484

21st Century

Babel, *Cildo Meireles*	489
Flower Thrower, *Banksy*	490
The Spire, *Ian Ritchie (Architect)*	491
Untitled (Bacchus), *Cy Twombly*	492
Untitled (I-IX), *Cy Twombly*	493

Contents

Wiringpa, *Simon Hogan*	494
Rise, *Wolfgang Buttress*	495
Little Girl with Teddy, *Sam Philip*	496
Miss Spring, *Yoshitomo Nara*	498
Reflection Model (Itsukushima), *Takahiro Iwasaki*	500
The Future, *Elmgreen & Dragset*	501
Bit. Fall, *Julius Popp*	503
Venus, *Jeff Koons*	505
Dialogue, *Lee Ufan*	506
Two Step, *Nina Chanel Abney*	507
Unearthed Leaves, *Sandra Mujinga*	509

er
14th Century

JOHN THE BAPTIST

My finger is addressing the higher realm
wherein night
has turned into midday, virulent echoes
blown from centuries past—
the dove's white wings

morbidity,
pearlescence

the underworld annihilated in one,
vast cosmic expanse,
where, at the center,
immortal sacrifice floods the stars.

The scroll I am holding anticipates the living Word:

love will conquer all hatred,
death will no longer transfix our gaze
in slumber never to be resurrected.

My silent countenance
is the expectation of One
who will transform the very ground
of existence, illuminate the crannies
of suffering

transfigure destiny
out of evil
into light.

1300, Byzantine Icon
British Museum, London

PIETÀ RÖTTGEN

Should his wounds drip over my thighs,
I'll hold him.
Should he bleed
into my heart,
I'll open like a flower awaiting an afternoon downpour.
Should he crumple further
into a weight that sinks below the plane
of tears,
even if the grit
in my throat makes me choke,
the gel in both eyes blackens midnight,
the fiber connecting my knees and womb
is severed,
I will,
despite the vain anticipation
of succor from ethereal realms,
at least,
embracing the inevitable commitment
of motherhood,
tend to his needs as he descends.

1300, German Sculpture
Rheinisches Landesmuseum, Bonn, Germany

GOLDEN BUDDHA OF SUKHOTHAI

Night—
the eternal distance filling with the brightest light.

The sea—
the salt filled expanse accommodating a diverse range
of living creatures.

A human eye—
a white ball absorbing every color that clings to birds, trees, reptiles,
and rain-soaked lineaments.

A beating heart—a center reflecting the same glow
as metallic skin reflecting a burning candle

the compassion
of an old monk and,
standing slightly to the side behind its parent's legs,
the awe of a child admitted at higher bequest.

Embodiment—

liquid sun distilled on earth.

14th Century,
Wat Traimit, Bangkok, Thailand

TRANSFIGURATION

Bleed
and it will glow,
open your mouth
and stars will pour forth,
stand erect
and the earth will burn beneath your feet

as the sky turns to mist,
gilt swords pierce the strata
where angels abide,
and dust,
forbidden to clump
in a handful, sparkles with intent
to illuminate each circumference,
drift beyond the clouds,
surprise the sun with raiment

embody

your presence

in our gaze.

1307, Duccio
National Gallery, London

THE DORMITION OF THE VIRGIN MARY

That final,
one,
untainted breath
deep as solitude filled with light

that flicker of an eyelid,
soft as a babe's need to touch mother's waist,
lingering
and stilling the water born to well

that last beat,
echoing with an angel's descent
into the rough
and ready human will to receive it,
dissipating like dandelion fluff
into mid-morning air

the vital sheath enclosing will
to survive like mist
on a mountain top receding into the blaze
at noon,
the blue that intensifies
then pales,
lifting to reveal the remains
of she
who took on the responsibility
of relieving woe

in this instance,
forgetful of their source in darkness,
transcendent to their own burst into pink flesh,
suddenly realizing they have no being
in substantial form
she doesn't feel.

1312, Giotto
Gemäldegalerie, Berlin, Germany

ST GEMINIANUS

I have only a staff
to guide you, pointing the way:

the Word incarnate.

I trust you can see the direction I offer,
illuminating the path between folly and death,
the soul's eclipse:

clarity new as morning,
vigilance bright as mountain snow,
a well deep as a moonless nights preceding slumber.

I have only the text written within divine hearing
to annihilate the bruise in your heart,
mystifying godlessness
with arabesques vaunted from clear scented heights:

the descent from Creation
to an iota caught up in love.

I'll trace every letter,
burning the dust on their darkness.

Will you pronounce them,
and reveal yourself on His plane?

1319, Simone Martini
Fitzwilliam Museum, Cambridge, England

THE GREAT EAST WINDOW

Should the dawn aim renewal
through the Virgin's breast,
the flame of her devotion
will color the pate
of a lowly soul kneeling in submission

should the eastern rays pour through a saint's visage,
it will light up the features
of a dour malingerer questing forgiveness

should the sun illumine His gaze,
it will reach a wounded penitent
on the floor.

For the breadth will gather every hue,
saturate the distance
between a blanched heart and bursting forth in paradise

the height manifest the reaches of boundless aspiration,
the translucence
of each panel, fluid
with inpouring grace and outward supplication,
bring the force
of identity

with He who made all light
into the darkness of the tomb.

1350, Gloucester Cathedral, Gloucester, England

THE MARRIAGE OF THE VIRGIN

In an ideal world, two will stay together
until that same real calls them together again
for Eternity.

In this world,
we can only hope that descent
into this world
will carry an inkling
of the other realm that will persist
until we are called.

In an ideal realm, the substance
of her heart
will meld with the texture
of his own.

In this world, although separated
by the tide and shifting seas,
we can only hope that where the light
from her breast meets the darkness
in his ribs,
and the blindness in her womb
is touched by the desire in his bones,
the unfolding of life's pattern
on the stretch

of mortal suffering
will bring forth the hardiest of fruit.

1380, Niccolo di Bonaccorso
National Gallery, London

WILTON DIPTYCH

Puissant body, tainted not
by excoriated witness encircling your heart,
reach toward me, and though a blade
of light, touch my crown

sentient mother,
feeling the throng of devotion
and obedience through your breast,
greet me with the softness in your eyes

bevy of adulation, transfixed
in the aura infusing each glazed lip,
burnished cheek and lid barely fluttering,
in the unadulterated air, foregoing pyres lit
on the outskirts of human strife,
tell me
I am worthy
of kneeling before you.

1395, English or French
National Gallery, London

15th Century

BIRD IN PLUM TREE

The earth's unlimited vision assumes equal power
to the unbounded creative:

bright leaves carved like a sword
and the instant,
not unlike the swoop
into pink and white,
a brush splays ink

speckled feathers,
the mood to procreate

pollen dust smearing a pointed beak,
the present recovered on silk
with the ageless craft of an artisan
indebted to the path of his forefathers

an eagerly penetrating eye,
an emerald bud imbued with the impetus

to flower

in spring.

1400s, Kano Kakusho
National Museum, Tokyo

DISH WITH DESIGN OF PINE TREES

Would you care to walk
in a landscape drenched in the darkest blue,
drift on a river white as clouds

under an above, melt
into the center
of the same white expanse

then let me lead you through a glaze
so bright
it reflects the light to your past lives,
to a silent, sure place
you would want to stay for a hundred years

unencumbered by the dazzle of a myriad
of colors,
to the uncomplicated contrast
where the gnarled trunk has no conflict
with the young leaves, the flowers
no contention with the odd weed

the sky,
pure as time losing its race
to arrive on the crest
of difference,
calming the curve

in the white

of your eye.

1403–23, Blue and White Jingdezhen Ware (Guanyao)China
Idemitsu Museum of Arts, Tokyo

MADONNA AND CHILD WITH ST ANNE

Arching Heaven beyond our seeing,
yet narrowing focus on a raindrop
and bubbles enshrining tepid air

descending where we bleed and taste the gums
of stale fish,
entering where a seer will succumb to black fields,
burnt husks,
and stalks winnowed by the river's edge

surfacing to gaze on a dandelion's heart,
centering near the bosom spreading love
in four directions:

lacerated flesh
and eyes mirroring the warmth in its sockets,
the zenith burgeoning with orisons,
the womb, now vacated,
no longer anticipating a stirring from the heights

lissome curves holding the embodied visitant

1424–25, Masaccio/Masolino
Uffizi Gallery, Florence, Italy

EXPULSION FROM THE GARDEN OF EDEN

Drench our bones with tears,
flay our once perfect skin,
with the sword that drives us from your arbor,
carve upon our heart the name
you spoke to us
at the beginning

when blood splotches appear,
and the desert wind rasps our hair
and stings our eyes,
invoke memories
of glades,
streams, languor,
and nonchalance.

What was it?

We can't look.

It is too far below our dreams.

1425, Masaccio
Brancaccio Chapel, Florence, Italy

MARY MAGDALENE'S SEA VOYAGE TO FRANCE

Upon vast,
unchartered waters I cross,
the gentle prow moving
without knowing who holds the helm

the wind,
fresh
as a gull's downward spiral filling my sail,
out of this world

indefinite horizons,
lustrous blue,
an anchor catching my naval.

Under green waves, translucent
as the earliest ever death,
I pass the fish swollen zone, scrape the bottom

objects of allurement entering my gaze,
glutinous lips mouthing refrains
of light starved ecstasy:

"Devour, devour,
until the core is exposed,
and eat it

savor the mellow taste of flesh that lives."

Up through bubbles popping and globules emerging,
opening and bubbles again,
air depleted lungs gasping for more
and more,
a freshwater spring rising through my bones

resume my way.

1432, Lucas Moser
The Magdalene Altar, St Mary Magdalene Church, Tiefenbronn, Germany

THE JOURNEY OF THE MAGI

May we dispense with the entourage
and alone face the wilderness
with an uncanny glow to penetrate our dreams,
only the subliminal,
certain conviction
we'll meet its embodiment

imminent
with arrival,
loosened from ethereal flame,
descending past the sun's molten eye,
the sap of trees,
congealed scent,
into the hardness of the earth

the acquisitive, sensual,
embittered throng that would despoil its utterance,
eyes blind vigilance

distant
from the source keeping each moment
in coherence
with the last

and the next,
hearts stifle rise and fall.

1433, Sassetta
Metropolitan Museum, New York

ARNOLFINI PORTRAIT

A particle
of my bone, a drop
of his blood fusing in earth patented sorrow

never sought in the shadows, immobile
as dust,
a hand resting upon a palm

whisps
of higher identity bound in the one new creature
we acknowledge as ours.

An inkling of her submission
to the deity who makes all things bloom,
a sliver of my intention
to amass wealth
swelling in her womb

the moon
and stars mirrored in a pair
of eyes that will look up in wonder.

Sand shifting along the riverbed,
oft visited crossroads at the foot of the woods:

an errantly chosen road passing through rubble
and sinking in mud,

an aura of diamantine light sublimating chance
to penetrating vision,
bell shaped flowers opening alongside the pathway

the union absorbing all a good life can give.

1434, Jan van Eyck
National Gallery, London

PORTRAIT OF A WOMAN WITH A WINGED BONNET

For a century,
I could frame the glint in your eye
with a blue sea

a millennium, taste your lips

a moment,
lose the horizon
in the silence separating my inertia laden heart
from your live beat fluctuating between the flight
of paradisial birds
and the robin's red breast exquisitely delineated
in the snow.

Foreign
to the manner you gaze
at entities forever benign
beyond the darkness over my shoulder,
dead light buries in ash

incalculable to worldly desire,
the hush cojoins an unsoiled bosom below
with refrains of heavenly singing above

lost to the carnal,
the unfathomable calm inheres in the center

of my studiousness
and your repose

each time we face one another.

1435, Rogier van der Weyden
Gemäldegalerie, Berlin, Germany

THE BAPTISM OF CHRIST

So distant from an open eye, the transparent tissue
of an immaculate body suspends in an instant
before my searching gaze

the dove,
consanguineous with white blood,
elevates where doom cannot penetrate

the descendant, foresworn to kinship,
surrenders to the earth
mute with clouded membrane, self absorption
born in its first breath,
a readiness to accede
to nonchalance twisted from concrete avowal

the water sprinkling
on His brow awakens a dormant fear
that, eventually, in the throes
of rejection,
He must submit to the flood brimming to the clouds

the tree, providing shade from a relentless,
broiling sun,
as if no one had ever plucked a leaf,
ushers a root in heavenliness finding a way
through the film which could,

if sight cranes an iris in disbelief,
retreat even further

in timelessness

no one will evince.

1437, Piero della Francesca
National Gallery, London

THE VISION OF SAINT EUSTACE

Cruel the teeth in a stag's thigh, maudlin
the wind through a rabbit's torn ear,
open the wound
in the figment bleeding through the sheen

erect my posture on a battle charger,
dark
the recess between the leaves
and haunted blades crunched underneath,
cerebral the light that denies proportion inside the pall:

bones
the size of an eyelid,
sallow droop
the verve of a brow.

It couldn't be the clutch at a child's windpipe,
the springing into regret

the fillip
of sentience descrying apotheosis:
"You can be great if you bow before stone"

the corrosive night
without sleep, the minotaur's slump
on purslane

the love is too great.

1438, Pisanello
National Gallery, London

SAINT LAWRENCE ENTHRONED WITH SAINTS COSMOS AND DAMIAN AND DEMOS

Egregious crime against your flesh,
but you poise on the threshold
extraneous to bitter lips

a godfather to the empty handed, a martyr
for evincing Scripture outside your robes.

Self-acclamation exacts desireful culmination,
but you stare into the heart that bled oceans
for us to rise upon

nobody has the power to intoxicate your serenity.

Imbued with an even more distant touch
of the Creator's will to persist,
a pagan demigod
entranced with his own fragrance
will carve the bones that accepted light

but acclimatised
with the supreme artist,
you expect,
albeit drenched in dust and clay,

to be brushed with the hues
only angelic being could radiate.

1440, Fra Filippo Lippi
Metropolitan Museum, New York

DAVID

Naked
before the Creator who entered every sinew,
I swallowed the fire immolating cowardice

alone
before the Maker
who accompanied me to the end,
unloosed concentrated grit into a speck
above his eyes

incumbent
over the giant
who would have killed me,
angled my bones
toward dead air brooding on his forehead,
eschewed toxin rising from his brain

enclosed in death's rattle,
absorbed manna drifting from a pink cloud,
quelled the beat
furiously demanding I retreat
into the shell of a child,
refuse to sever a head, drain fluid into the earth

quail before the affirmation:

you have destroyed the impediment
to High and Mighty continuation
in the bones and blood of a servant.

1445c, Donatello
Bargello National Museum, Florence, Italy

THE ANNUNCIATION

Like a petal in night wind fluttering against skin
and membrane,
gently breaking the will
whose fluctuations can hardly perceive my entry,
I have arrived:

You will bear a child
who will proceed from a realm
fine as the features
on your priceless image

consanguineous with beasts
of the field, taste the droplets
an earthly man inebriated with need
to pulse under the same sun
for eons
the blood that cannot rise
can sip

in the instant of conception,
expand the parameters
of your universe
until the throes limiting perception
rinse in cloud light

enter your womb.

1449, Fra Angelico
Convent of San Marco, Florence, Italy

LANDSCAPE

There is only
so far we can go

mist rises above perception.

We can concentrate
on effort required
to move an immovable object, the cleft
in rock where water spumes,
the gaunt trunk
and spreading leaves

but
even with eyes devouring the texts
of the ancients, penetrating observation
of the morning sun bleeding into roots,
the moon's honest light touching a bough
and filtering into sap,
we shall never find the perfect brush
to tease out the emptiness
which swallows every hush, limpid pool
and fallow

pours forth

in a flurry

of birdsong.

1450, Dai Jin
National Gallery of Victoria, Melbourne

JOHN THE BAPTIST

An emissary announcing the irreconcilable opposites:

damnation
or resurrection.

An initiate realizing the future:

a Master who will die following the path.

An ambassador
from silence inducing the mind corrupted in darkness
to hear the Word:

surreal candour breaking in like sunlight upon a pond.

An instrument
of deliverance foreshadowing life's inevitable inception:

movement from despair in selffull self-reflection
to unsullied existence

a changed world.

1451, Antonio Vivarini
Kunsthistorisches Museum, Vienna

AGONY IN THE GARDENS

Otherworldly: the certainty
you could have done anything.
Internment:
netherworldy silence blanketing sobs.
Slumber:
unearthly absence relieving connection
with lips smearing an upturned forehead.
Dreams:
night corroding outer limits,
angels drifting on limpid air,
drunken realms opening a bloody maw,
the blazing sword battling a dragon.
Purpureal aura: the stain
of annihilation.
Embodiment: the detached
yet burnished graft
with cleft palate, eyelessness,
and burning limbs

thrumming in your backbone

willingness

to cry

when we deserted you.

1455, Andrea Mantegna
National Gallery, London

SAINT SEBASTIAN

Should I reconstitute flesh in marble,
you won't feel the brute entry
nor the points draining your life force.
Should I destroy the structure that incarcerates the means
to climb out of embodiment,
eyes can freely turn in the direction
of One
who supplants iniquity with impermeability.
If I reify transcendent light, heat
will glisten on muscle,
shine on every exposed feature,
irradiate the bond tying you to the earth.
If I uphold nakedness toward the source
of ecstasy,
base intent shall reach the sphere
of the Artist

with a touch brushing away all tears,
manifest the plane

where pain

can't penetrate

1456, Andrea Mantegna
Kunsthistorisches Museum, Vienna

PORTRAIT OF A YOUNG WOMAN

Silent water fills the gulf
between the dead lining under my feet
and the moon's reflection,
lumina dance in the vista from your eyes
to light forming a perfect circle above dark contours.

Numb chords accrue in the distance
between the beat
in my chest and the thrush's song,
loud
and clear in the evening grove

rapture enthuses the space between your ear
and Heaven's refrain entering the throat
of a gifted recipient,
albeit held to the earth
by languor,
and ready to touch the clouds
in one unperturbed flight.

Forewarned
of status,
endless hope reaches from a pauper
to firelight diffusing heat
in cloistered air

delicate
as a leaf fluttering in autumn\s chill,
anticipation rises with fingers
to your throat.

1465, Antonio or Piero del Pollaiuolo
Gemäldegalerie, Berlin

HUNT IN THE FOREST

I am under no illusion
the prey won't be torn apart, the smell
of blood saturate the night air,
dogs gnaw the bones tossed aside

fur will lay heavily on a woman's shoulders,
teeth, perchance, string around a neck,
head
and dead eyes gaze benignly from a wall

we are the warriors,
the undoubted masters
of pursuit, the owners
of clamor,
dictators over earth's fauna

blind distance is ours
to fill,
moonlight ours to traverse the land by

an animal,
disrupted from its normal pattern
of behavior,
ours

to kill.

1465, Paolo Uccello
Ashmolean Museum, Oxford, England

ST JEROME IN HIS STUDY

I work with patience
to counter the evil one's incursions,
resisting the temptation
to scribble feelings
of wonder and joy.

I have no desire
to cede consciousness
to an agitated body, recognizing all worry
is but evidence of a misguided aim harboring passion.

I contemplate intensely the trials
of the Sufferer,
deriving principles of consequence
from coherence born in serenity.

I write
to elucidate qualities sustained in equilibrium:

the ideal fathomed
at its source,
attunement to the pinnacle, making every affirmation
definitive of one perfectly meant signification:

One letter, Alpha, Father,
virtue, forms the beginning

one letter, Omega, Holy Order,
constitutes the end.

1474, Antonello da Messina
National Gallery, London

DAMA DEL MAZZOLINO

Will I forget who I am,
break my bond with decent behaviour
and fling my body at his feet

with dignity of composure,
take his hand and offer condolences
for having reached the plane
which found us together in matter?

Will I hold
to my breast the rose
which signifies time transfused
with the blood
of future generations bearing fruit
I can count on as my progeny

or simply

express the love

I long for?

1475, Andrea del Verrocchio
Bargello Palace, Florence, Italy

PORTRAIT OF A YOUNG MAN

Close the door
and allow me to reflect
on the present:

her refusal to trust my advances,
her denial
to drink integrity

the rose crushed on the path,
the weeping sky refusing to stifle the clouds,
the blackbird swallowing drops
quenching its song

the past:

my ardor,
my anticipation,
unbeknownst to her heart,
I would plunder her joy and instill mine
in its stead

the narrow laneway
where I pressed her against stone,
the glint
in her eye where I fathomed my demeanor
would be etched, the gasp
as I drained the softness of a dream

the future:

an elderly man cringing in the inexorable advance
of grey hair and broken fingernails

bloodstains
on my pillow,
grey lids folding into sleep

a cell resonant

with solitary breath needing another coat
of whitewash.

1477, Domenico Ghirlandaio
Ashmolean Museum, Oxford, England

SULTAN MEHMET II SMELLING A ROSE

For a second, Heaven wavers under my nostrils,
the sky's azure drenches my speech,
the clouds,
rain and blossoming on the hillside
clog my senses with delight.

For a lifetime,
blood will flow and nourish my eyes,
light
burn a track through my brain,
velocity turn
and wheel until it subsides.

Beyond the tomb
where my body
will rest,
fragrant petals will unfold,
the center divulge the secret attracting insects
to darkness,
the ineffably distant hint
of immortality mingle with air,
color
and dust

slay the rising thought of self-importance.

1480, Ottoman
Topkapi Palace Museum, Istanbul, Turkey

THE BIRTH OF VENUS

One breath closer to our shore,
you'll shower us with blossom,
paint the vernal undergrowth
with a hue reflecting the abode
reticent to wake as a morning dream,
the tint on leaves
with a hint reminiscent of your bright eyes,
brows held upward
fearful of demise
with scented peach petal skin

as you are blown
to the cries formed in our breasts,
singularly naked beauty exposed to divine desire
and will,
you'll form an image
of embodied light

the translucent first-born manifesting in flesh
and bone, enabling our hearts

to seek another

in union.

1485, Sandro Botticelli
Uffizi Gallery, Florence

THE ANNUNCIATION, WITH SAINT EMIDIUS

Slice veins in black leaves,
cut through stone,
smolder the air
in the prison tortured by reticence,
rephrase the meaning of hard light

penetrate to blood and fiber,
reach the center of time
and worldly sustenance,
coruscate like embers from centuries past
on manna forming a crust on dew

repeat,
in a ray set to blind the seer of wit,
the ineffable to the scholar,
the misunderstood to holy men,
the elusive to the righteous
who, furnished with the text
of the ages,
ponder its depths
for the one, ultimate revelation.

1486, Carlo Crivelli
National Gallery, London

ST. AUGUSTINE

Fortuitously,
not only do you have your eye on the spiraling descent
of an angel into the clouds,
but your feet touch the heavy earth
with each sure step

not only
can you evince the strictures
of the Word condescending to reach
into the black matter under our hearts,
but clasping grains of wheat in your horny palm,
feel its potential to ripen into nourishment
fit for a gangling figure

not only do you sense the sun's brightness,
radiant like the source of light incarnate,
illuminating the way
to take when the body fails
and pores clog with fear of the end

but on an ordinary day,
when the rain trickles down your neck
and mud squelches between your toes,
point out with an outstretched finger

the path
to a dry little tavern at the end of the street.

1487, Carlo Crivelli
The National Museum of Western Art, Tokyo, Japan

AUTUMN LANDSCAPE

Empty my youth
in steam and ice water,
bring the moon's bright sheen
to rest on my shoulder.

I can only rejoin.

Let me perch
like a wounded crow on stunted growth,
drain sap from my haunches

the wind, low across the stubble,
trace an airy zero on my spine.

To which I'll respond.

Sallow the droop in your lids, pale
the light in your countenance,
bereft of a glint in your sad, black eyes.

I must appear just like you.

1496, Sesshu
National Museum, Tokyo

16th Century

TAKING A LUTE TO VISIT A FRIEND

The first note will bring comfort
to a jaded warrior

the second,
a moment
of red life to mordant blood

a flurry
pronounced with memory
of turbulent youth,
the vigor
we stretched over chasms
and jagged edges

in search
of the tiger's leap toward our spears,
our venture
with no thought of losing foothold
through a vague,
crystalline edged opening—

the foresight of our forever.

1500, Jiang Song (attributed to)
Hayward Gallery, London

THE PEDDLER

A lonely man ought sometimes satisfy his loins.
What will come of it?
Nothing much.
An exclamation in pleasure, a release,
a burst of bodily dew.
Then what?
The same dreary course
until the next dingy house waves soiled linen
from an upper window.

1500, Hieronymus Bosch
Museum Boijmans Van Beuningen, Rotterdam

THE ENTOMBMENT

We can only know
that the earth will receive its own,
swallow every grain
of sweat, flush of pink,
and fully formed bone
that congeals in a sure step
and soothing touch.

How
can we possibly know,
that given the spark channeled from perfection,
animation will resurface from the feet
to the head,
vitality descend from pigment free lucence
to a blind swirl,
luster form the eyes

midnight, devoid of sense and movement,
we expect will surround him,
as it will us,
stay within a tiny slice
under his soul?

Please don't go.

1500, Michaelangelo
National Gallery, London

SELF PORTRAIT

On the surface it would seem
I have usurped Christs inhabitation,
withholding,
though, the entire descent,
taking for myself
the faculties that address humanity

foresight:

what will happen
to every soul
when it reaches the shores of judgement

benevolence:

what will circle in the spine
when Centaurus reaches flesh
and transforms into its likeness

and, breaching the shadows
that surround a heart,
gentleness:

what opens the Moon's face
and inspires a brush
to apportion life to every pursed lip
and steadfast eye

yet, tantamount
to a beggar who asks the fount
to grace with emolument
fit for hardly touching His invisible cloak,
I am fully aware
that any gift
of acumen thrown my way
is only an ounce,
or even less, of his weight,
weightlessness even so,
into the taut fingers tempering utmost inclination
to reach incalculable depths,
inestimable heights

purity of vision.

1500, Albrecht Dürer
Alte Pinakothek, Munich

SAMSON AND DELILAH

The first lock will drain him
of vigor,
the second—
the propensity to greatness,
the third—
the eye to see evil,
and after that
one after the other,
blunt as dead grass

lank,
with the odor of stale perfume

his manhood.

1500, Andrea Mantegna
National Gallery, London

DOGE LEONARDO LOREDAN

Graze my forehead with a spear
and I'll retaliate just as earnestly
with blunt sword and gilded edge,
strive to delete the air above my head
and I'll engulf you in boiling glass

sacrilegiously,
carve your symbols
reminiscent of the devil's scrawl
on our vestments,
our pavements,
our columns
and, drawing fire from the bosom
of hell if need be,
I'll melt your eyes and sear your brain

our land
is the deification
of fathomless will to own destiny,
our rites
the manifestation
of patterns only the divine could conceive

our temper, incarnating in flesh,
the distillation
of purity drawn from ice on winter nights,

high borne snow on the mountains
we'd erase in the storm of contrition.

We are under the auspices
of the highest,
most sovereign Lord.

1501, Giovanni Bellini
National Gallery, London

MONA LISA

If I had it in my power I'd exhume the face of an angel
and render it unearthly,
transpose the flight
of a bee
with the undulation of a heavenly being

substitute the flame
in a rising star
for the fleck in an iris,
adhere an eyelash to the tree
that stands over the stream in Paradise

in the furrows
of deprivation, instill Ambrosia
upon which the Gods sup at evening,
raise the moisture into Aphrodite's veins

awaken bodiless slumber
in light dawning on the first morning
on an ancient land preceding the birth of our own,
effect emptiness
in the glance toward the openness
I'll close in emptiness
that gave birth to the first human breath

in frost,
which will never dissipate

until I drench the sunset before I sleep
and the hue which saturates a climbing red rose
with the blood
in your veins,
pour sunlight into the yellow butterflies
descending behind me

and you'll smile.

1503, Leonardo Da Vinci
The Louvre, Paris

PIPER AND DRUMMER

We can evoke the balm
of Gilead, the fluttering certainty
of a dove poised to descend

evince the legions
of wilderness beasts
who succumbed to the soft hands
of the sun god himself,
the tympany accompanying the rise
and fall
of ghost's passage through earthy atmosphere

flow
in unison,
and in harmony with Saturn's dour countenance,
rephrase the moon's encirclement
of a stationary center
and the burst
of manna into our sphere

in the manner
of Pan, long for an open ear.

Treat us to repair you, Lord

1505, Albrecht Dürer
Wallraf-Richartz Museum, Cologne, Germany

THE ANSIDEI MADONNA

First step—
leave the harsh core
in a hollow.

Second—
assume cloud light
will penetrate your brain,
mystical madrigals follow in accompaniment.

Once more—
as the furnace illuminates a snow laden breast
and feathered wings soar into nebulous skies,
the rain decreasing a soul's wandering zest
will glance
off an upturned brow melding with the skies.

Thereupon—invited
by sirens to surpass their glee,
like ice on a white flame,
a nought
on a series of unending value

in the prescient, lit up penetration
of an adoring eye,
melt finally,
as would a virgin's reluctance
in the heat of her truly found,

once in a lifetime,
only
and solely hers,
lover.

1505–7, Raphael
National Gallery, London

POPE JULIUS II

Somehow,
I doubt you will be receptive
to my request
to saturate your bones
with the being that orders,
commands
and directs.

you will elude my vow
to capture your majesty,
pomp, and splendour,
affirming you as the agent
of infallible dictation from the fountainhead—

the veritable purveyor of secrets,
who will transform humanity
in the image of the unfolding of life becoming light,
neither seen
or sensed by ordinary men
in the conclave known in our time

you
will never let me capture the greatness
that lies within,
as it counters the mistakes
of heathen—

an organism inflaming incorrigible doubt,
lassitude
and inebriation in flesh so sordid to your touch.

No.

You will not inhume indignity
and present me with your inner fire,
but with the man who has failed to stem the rising flow
of wickedness

who has only memory
of a frustrated goal to address the people
who depend on him for guidance.

1508, Raphael
National Gallery, London

THE TEMPTATION OF SAINT ANTHONY

We'll pulp the eyes bulging in gloom.

The gladsome burst of Christ
will enlighten the sockets.

We'll tear the lips from your mouth.

I have nothing important to say.

Your heart will be a fine place to dwell

lizard skin the coverlet, black sap the blood,
cicada's whirring in the pulse.

Love dissolved shadows centuries
before flesh began to beat.

Bones shall point to the manger on fire,
crinkling skin
and melting veins.

Tears will quench the flames.

1512–15, Matthias Grünewald
Isenheim Altar, Unterlinden Museum, Colmar, France.

DYING SLAVE

All my vigor will dissipate,
tenderness in my limbs suffuse,
not with the moon's sultry glow
or even Saturn's pale emanation at midnight,
but within damp earth, a snails trail,
and
in the vacant hole between marrow long gone
and the yellowing bone left to lie on a salt flat,
the elemental question that preceded my embodiment,
which at first glance glistens with the health
of a god.

"Has entrapment been allocated
to my first breath
because we fell eons ago,
or is it,
in this and only instance
with no foreknowledge of why?"

1513, Michelangelo
Louvre, Paris

BELEM MADONNA AND CHILD
(OUR LADY OF THE GRAPES)

Wipe vine leaves on salt blanched eyes,
fill us with juice as the cold drains our veins

the wear in your face enough to enclose manna.

Polish our skin with the aura untouched
by the highest wave,
in the breath from your shadow
loosen our bond with bedrock:

an orison issuing forth as words to numb a trachea
as the depths numb a kick to the surface.

Quell the storm with light from your brow,
hold us above the rage as you hold the child

momentum quelled,
the song of bad blood silenced

the vast ocean alive with teeth and spikes
no longer a distance
between the brawn

in our limbs
and the milk in your breasts.

1514, Sculpture
Tower of Belem, Lisbon, Portugal

CHRIST SHOWING HIS WOUNDS

Swallow me in your gaze,
wipe away the sweat
on my forehead

lazily dull
not attuned to a pale aura on your crown,
stolid
not assured
of morning light in your iris

still,
I'll wash your blood with my tears,
expect you'll come closer
to the steps
I am taking towards you.

Touch the skin, put your finger in the holes

warm
not cold, open not closed,
drained of fluid
yet full

a tingling
through to your bones,
a long piercing cry evincing the will
to walk, advance nearer

declare sovereignty over flesh

and carnal desire
through to your core.

1515–1520, German Sculpture
Louvre, Abu Dhabi

THE CRUCIFIXION OF CHRIST

Sweltering night, deny us this one glimmer,
and we'll be hemmed in for eons

take from us this one,
clear mote
in a black dream,
and we shall dream
in its center

subtract
from our midst
the one instance
of untainted blood

and we will drown.

1515, Matthias Grünewald
Kunstmuseum, Basel, Switzerland

ASSUMPTION OF THE VIRGIN

No longer have I an earthly home

my abode has no connection
with the chaos.

My presence isn't needed where followers fade
and insects crawl over bare limbs

I have it within
to escape coarse skin that smells of sulfur.

I am not required to spend time holding a mirror
which reflects lines of woe and worry

the light transfusing my body with ardor
is enough for my blood to sense lightness
and my heart stop beating,
yet still live with the pulse of His love.

The radiant sunrise,
the mystical chalice pouring liquid into parched throats,
the ephemeral dance
of elfin waifs caught up in winds heralding arrival
from eternity,
is naught
compared with the absence
of all that leads to the grave

in one swift uplift, I'll approach his demand
that affliction,
ultimately,
cease.

1515, Titian
Basilica S. Maria Gloriosa dei Frari, Venice, Italy

RESURRECTION

Every possible taste,
every conceivable moment
of happiness, every instant of delight,
pain, temptation,
and animal feeling was mine to luxuriate in,
dismiss, or value
as an instant
of your suffering
when I touched down on the furrows of the earth

now,
in one blinding flash of supernal light,
they will dissipate

and I

rise above them.

1516, Matthias Grünewald
Isenheim Altapiece, Unterlinden Museum, Colmar, France

LANDSCAPE WITH A FOOTBRIDGE

Transcendence bears no relation to the heart
until the ineffable,
the eternal beyond, the imperceivable
translate into the hidden behind each murmur

stone,
leaf, and bark subsume to hierarchical order
at the nadir
unless,
with a glance at the light bleeding though my fingers,
are lifted to their source illuminating each crack,
vein, and splinter.

A mortal
will not taste the free flight of constancy beyond the grave
until the abyss is overarched with a permanent structure—

candor,
love, and reception of a gift

the darkest spot will not infer the existence
of the immortal glow preceding life
unless,

with an intricate pattern surpassing the rocks below,
I cross warily with a gift in return.

1518–20, Albrecht Altdorfer
National Gallery, London

AN ALLEGORY ON THE SACK OF ROME

If I had the tools,
I would protect her
from lasciviousness and cruelty

with unerring speed,
raise her from the midst
of turmoil,
rescue her pure milk
from despoliation,
free her ripe breasts
from the hands that would grasp them

when the church has turned a blind eye
to the corruption at the center,
lift into the dew melding with light,
translate her fear of enslavement
into the succor
of the clouds floating on angel's breath
in advance of restoration:
the perfect heart
beating beyond the point
that would puncture it.

1530, (Maiolica Plate), Francesco Xanto Avelli
Art Gallery of New South Wales, Sydney

PORTRAIT OF THE MERCHANT GEORG GIESE

I'll identify my spine
with the rock upon which a fortune
can accumulate,
gold
with the kernel that glows unabated,
accoutrements with each organ sustaining a vital,
self-respecting order of existence.

Not only will I conquer greed,
an abundance
over and above the life force
valued for its projection
into the morass of wheeling and dealing,
excess deflating creative intent in the profession
I am drawn to,
but will sublimate accumulation for its own sake
to the realization:

business must prosper
if the wellbeing of others,
who depend on me
for sustenance,
shall swell in the richness of my heart
and the solidity of my bones

the bodies,
which coalesce in the foundation of the city,
avoid lying in the gutter
like the pauper bundled in rags

swallowed in rain.

1532, Hans Holbein the Younger
Gemäldegalerie, Berlin

ECCE HOMO

Take note of the official,
how he, in blue raiment,
offers up a man shorn of dignity.

Regard the Savior,
how he submits to the verdict of the mob.

Imbibe the night, how it numbs the heart
and blossoms disorder,
now that he is taken from us
to die.

I see you, good Christ, I see you,
and trust
I will relinquish the desire
to persuade you to remain suffering,
now that you are to go.

1543, Titian
Kunsthistorisches Museum, Vienna

WINTRY TREES

I cling to the belief
I will revive, form buds,
and break into new leaf.
Even as the cold creeps deeply into my pith,
the stars dim light barely touches living lining,
and the crows settle maddingly raucously
on my gaunt limbs,
I am well aware that the steam running by
will proliferate with spawn,
the knots in my trunk glisten with sap,
and I'll make it through the winter.

1543, Wen Zhengming
Hayward Gallery, London

COSIMO 1 DE 'MEDICI IN ARMOR

Fortune finds no friendship in weakness

the outward gaze,
metallic to its core,
penetrates the haze
unto the deference returning in swathes.

Mildness militates against a sovereign's dream

blue castle dust forms a stronghold loftier than Etna,
transparent arcs cross the Alps,
feet land in white grape juice.

Colonnades
are built for the mighty,
not the feeble

metal plates staunch the red flow,
a point meets the fluid in a combustible head,
armor protects a staunch heart.

1545, Agnolo Bronzino
Art Gallery of New South Wales, Sydney

PORTRAIT OF A YOUNG MAN AS DAVID

Have I the stamina and fortitude of a youth
who would sever a gross head from the shoulders of a giant,
the courage
of a young man who would face the onslaught
of a godless throng

and,
with the simple skill gifted unto a lithe body,
embed a hard obstacle
into the center of thoughtlessness

would I,
when the clouds dark
as Hades descend upon the murky waters,
sustain an inkling of ardor
that would penetrate their breasts
and stun the movement in their bones?

The artist
will reveal me truly as I am:

a worthy successor to a king above all lords.

1555, Tintoretto
The National Museum of Western Art, Tokyo

GREAT ROCKERY

A poet may wander with the clouds
till he freezes in northern extremities,
peer into the surface
of an ancient pond
and count his teeth with glee

allow the summer to pour into his head,
and when every lineament
is baked into a sheen resembling the pottery
he studied in a barely upright hall,
count the days between him
and a predecessor
who,
predisposed to the same ruminations,
joins his words
with the one melodious outpouring

simply
under the shadow of a towering rock,
saturate with silence.

1559, Pan Yunduan
Yu Yuan Gardens, Shanghai, China

SAMSON SLAYING PHILISTINES

I found you with intent to disarm my nation.
I could sense your feral longing
to alter our path with One
who enables our blood to flow.
I could hear you sniveling at night,
meaning to goad us into flight.

I will smear you on the desert,
and castrate your stinking brood.

I will bludgeon you to a pulp.

1562, Giovanni Bologna
Victoria and Albert Museum, London

HARVESTERS

If we can, we'll ensure every ear is collected,
every sheaf stacked neatly,
every bundle hoisted on our shoulders
to be carried,
stored,
and eventually pulverized
into the form that becomes nourishment
for our hearts,
glands,
and sufferance enabling the cycle
to persist year after year.

For without strength nothing will be produced,
without rest strength won't be reenacted,
without reenactment
the village will die,
without the village
we'll live alone

on the outside
and not within

on the path through black stubble,
grey blossom,
and bleak skies.

1565, Pieter Bruegel the Elder
Metropolitan Museum of Art, New York

NOBLEMAN BETWEEN ACTIVE AND CONTEMPLATIVE LIFE

For one moment
you could see yourself
as a scholar pursuing the wisdom of the ages,
reflecting on Scripture
to determine how sages conducted the search
to find the sublime light
at the apex

an ascetic dispensing with the nighttime call
of the flesh,
submitting to silence
from which the fruits of vast ephemeral kingdoms emanate:

rhythm in consonance
with earnest breath surpassing worldly need,
enlightened love,
like nectar flowing from heavenly blossom,
reaching the heart

or,
invigorated by the sword glinting in dawn light,
a fully armed servitor conquering the charlatan
who'd render the population destitute
and the inebriated waif forever incumbent
in the fallow that never dries out

in the city's center,
when the bells ring in the tower,
facing the enemy's attack on innocence
and traps to ensnare the helpless

when evening firelight enhances the features
of a beauty's readiness to submit,
loosening her robes easily and softly,
until slumber erases any vestiges of pain
and wounds received from protecting her good name.

May the lord
help you
to choose in which bed to lie.

1575, Paolo Veronese
National Gallery of Victoria, Melbourne

ABDUCTION OF A SABINE WOMAN

Grow red eyes on while tabula,
steep earlobes in sticky nectar.

Stop them!

Bloat gonads in gruel,
plant fistula in decaying meat.

Stop them!

Prise lips with a carving knife,
drain pellucid milk
from oversized glands.

Stop them!

Raise solid perfume on contorted shoulders,
taste fear in grimy armpits,
embed nakedness
with drool sought by goddesses
in the firmaments.

Carry me to destiny!

1579, Giambologna
Loggia dei Lanzi, Florence, Italy

VENUS AND ADONIS

Out of the timeless realm she'll find a shadow
and wait

caress his lobes and fingers, entwine
like a vine, bleed him of nous
to picture flesh carved in siren's tryst

plea with darkness
to relieve suffering in the atmosphere
of mutual affection,
cauterize the pulse impounding light
in limbs and ardor in the hunt.

With no resolve to see an erroneous future avoidable,
he'll withdraw into lost realms,
squash black eggs and chase blue flies,
until sapping his vital strength,
turning her gaze to the mindless shell,
she'll address it with syrupy tones:

I need you. I can only have you,
touch you, and will surrender only to you
my body

numb your faculties, provide you with pleasure
so satisfying you'll give up every bead
of your life force

bring fruit in my bosom for eternity.

1595, Bartholomeus Spranger
Kunsthistorisches Museum, Vienna

17th Century

CHRIST DRIVING THE TRADERS FROM THE TEMPLE

Before caretakers eschewed responsibility—

a funicular burst
into the plane of matter,
largesse born in glittering light

at the center—

a calm eye,
taut veins

the Word ready to command:

Indignity will perish
in the swathe of a hand,
there will be no corrupt sessions in this temple

Mammon has no right to ply gratuitous need
for augmentation
where fellowship,
the one, final principle,
has been achieved
in the point unifying humanity
with the cosmic power

that will destroy
any attempt to subvert it.

1600, El Greco
National Gallery, London

CHRIST APPEARING TO ST PETER ON THE APPIAN WAY

Sweat blood
with me,
human,
feel the core tear,
the heart burst,
and the spleen pop from its place.

Is this too much to ask?

Feel the flesh tear from your thighs,
the brain rattle in its shell,
the wheeze confine to your face
and lips.

Are you prepared to wallow in the black river?

The promise is
that light will drench the wounds,
heat absorb spilled fluid,
an aura golden in hue,
constant in envelopment,
all pervasive
in penetrating to the depths of Satan's cares,
will,
if you embody the same scission
from sanity I must endure,

persuade Heaven to leave its door ajar
just as the torture enters its penultimate phase.

Why are you hesitating?

1601–2, Annibale Carracci
National Gallery, London

WINTER LANDSCAPE WITH BIRD TRAP

Eventually, ice will melt
and the rivers flow,
the snow recede
and buds open on bare twigs

but for the moment
cradled in cold,
we'll submit to the freeze,
crows caw lustily
at the thought of a tidbit left on white sills,
children dance
upon the hard surface
an iron spike can never penetrate

the village maestro,
with fingers frozen blue,
put away his harp,
and with the glee of a youngster
wary to miss the holes
that could swallow him unto the eternal depths,
skate past the girl,
who only last year,
when the frigid haze broke the will of a servant
to tend to his master's hearth,
gave birth to a child ,
which, despite her mother's swaddling her
in lambswool

and breathing her own warmth
onto her failing chest,
never saw the next bright winter
thronged with mirth.

1601, Pieter Breughel the Younger
The National Museum of Western Art, Tokyo

THE SUPPER AT EMMAUS

Deep
as the succor from timelessness,
does the ethereal countenance gainsay the wound
that bled into the earth,
a gentle wind
through each vein temper the resonance
from the fatal blow plunging into the depth
of agony

the body,
which has been delivered,
ready
to rise again,
entrance vision?

Christ reign within dark slumber
where sinners die,
reluctant to face him

or not?

1601, Caravaggio
National Gallery, London

DAVID WITH THE HEAD OF GOLIATH

My voice
is but the dulcet slur of a youth,
my curls the barely emerging growth
out of childhood,
my skin the unblemished contours
that reflect the pale gentleness of my mother

yet
my demeanor
the resolute cast of a warrior
who, alone, untutored,
bereft of experience,
illicitly carved
as an underling
by the great thinkers presupposing direct access
to the will of the almighty,
reveals obedience

the soft light that glowed within my skull
and urged me to sever the head of an adversary

my forthright stance,
sharp

as the edge
of a bloodied sword manifesting his prize.

1606, Caravaggio
Kunsthistorisches Museum, Vienna, Austria

BLACK-CAPPED KINGFISHER

Long grass will hide claws
and beak,
river haze devour every feather,
reeds obscure flecks of white

I'll penetrate to the shadow under his wings.

Flowers will surround the timeless stance,
tendrils enclose the night staining his skull,
leaves cancel any glimpse of red rim
and black socket

steady as the bough covering his perch,
silent
as the dawn chasing the vestiges
of moonlight
from a tail, perceptive
as the clear eye ever watchful
for a silver flash below,
I'll color plumage with the life
that will burst forth
when an impulse to dive seizes him.

C 1610, Mughal
National Gallery of Victoria, Melbourne

ELEVATION OF THE CROSS

Give us one more ounce
of matter
to lift bone and brawn upright
where it can sink again
into the dull air we breathe.

Provide us with gristle,
muscle
and pumping blood
to erect one who fanatically conceives divinity
as his mantle

now revealed
merely
as flesh glistening as ours.

Afford us the skill to effect crudely sawn timber
as a fitting epitaph
for one who,
constrained by the heat coaxing out globules
of sweat and cold solidifying droplets
on a forehead,
will merely dissipate
in the clouds

meld with the sand beneath our feet
and,

in a climax known to man,
woman
and child at the end,
beg for alleviation.

1610, Rubens
Cathedral of our Lady, Antwerp, Belgium

QUR'AN COMMISSIONED BY SULTAN 'ABDULLAH II AL SA'ADI

Should a circle diminish to a point,
what could expand
to touch the circumference
it left?
An intricate pattern?

And if this were to dissolve in the fervor of loss,
what could ascend
to take its place?
The color gold?

And if that were to contract so far
that an eye could no longer perceive its ineffable pointlessness,
what is left to fill the void?
Could it be the conception
that they all belong together
and enhance each other's reality

just as the skill, wisdom,
love and obedience coalesce
to produce that which will last
as a totality
on the one page dedicated to the Holy Text.

1616, Louvre, Abu Dhabi

THE WATERING PLACE

Blood will provide no succor
when thirst begs to be slaked,
brine only sting the eyes
when tears need to be washed away,
plant juice stain our lips
when untainted droplets are deemed necessary
to infuse a bad taste,
dilute the sweet liquid
which has no qualms in breaking an oath
with the higher powers that descend
and rise into pools
that reflect our sorrow
and descend again into our hearts

clear in us,
nourished

where we wait for sunrise
to appear.

1620, Rubens
National Gallery, London

NEPTUNE AND TRITON

The conch tastes like raw salt
on my lips

I'll blow until the moon hears its ascent.

The sea swirls toward my abdomen

I'll subdue it with iron and flesh.

The tide garners pace
and thrusts toward the headland

it still pursues its course
irrespective of our indomitability.

1622, Gian Lorenzo Bernini
Victoria and Albert Museum, London

AESOP

Gather around me
fine people
and I'll let on
what I think
you must savor.

If you cry wolf over and again
when no wolf is present,
a wolf eventually will appear
and one's cry for help will go unanswered.

The wolf will devour your flock,
decimate your kids

and at the end of the day,
when the sunset pours red over your domain,
you will hear a growl
in your heart.

1625, Jusepe de Ribera
Art Gallery of New South Wales, Sydney

TWO OLD MEN DISPUTING

What I think you must appreciate
is that the universe holds more secrets
than we can possibly fathom.
Have we lived before?
Are we only given one chance
to make amends with the Creator,
or is blind chance
the only cause
at the root of suffering?

You say that the one life is all we need
to cultivate a full and worthy path,
we have all the faculties
to ground the search in inevitable resolution.
But I am not sure.
On misty mornings when the windows are open
and dreams drift in from netherworlds
and otherworlds beyond my ken,
I can see the deeds
I have wrought
long before this body screamed as an infant,
and long before
I can look you in the eyes
and bring forth my deepest concern:

Would that I had the answer to the riddle
to redeem our plight

and carry us toward the future anew,
purified, I would accord to the Word
the highest principle humbly feeling could rise to.

Do you suppose
we could ever trust our notion
to relieve out frailty

or humbly accept our weakness
this time around.

1628, Rembrandt
National Gallery of Victoria, Melbourne

YASODA NURSING THE CHILD KRISHNA

Is that a tear?
Wipe it with a soft, clean cloth.
A shadow?
Tease it
from his brow with deft fingers.
A tight muscle?
Soften it with warmth from a breast.

Along with an opening blossom,
unfold his hand and tickle the interior.

Could that be a fly?
Dissuade it from landing with a short breath.
Moisture on lips?
Kiss it before it dissolves.

The surrender
to sleep?
Make no movement
as the stars change place
with sunlight,
the voice of the mountain stills the waves,
flocks settle on high boughs,
cattle lie down on dew drenched fields.

The cosmos will await an open eye.

C 1630, Bhagavata Purana Manuscript
National Gallery of Victoria, Melbourne

THE CROSSING OF THE RED SEA

Shake the dust off our feet

entombed in blood,
the nemesis staunched the flow of life
before we knew servility
and desperate striving to remember an unfettered past.

Expect no mercy

if you follow,
the depths will swallow every spear,
chariot, and smooth skinned warrior
who deigns to think
we belong to their fold.

Raise our eyes to the firmament

anticipate that at any moment,
the force that brought all creatures into existence
will cleave the waters,
inundate all things the mortal bleeds,
the woman fainting in agony of childbirth,
the infant whimpering in her arms
fearful of lack of nourishment

but the lord, over every facet of our lives
and intake of breath,
will protect the humanity that belongs to him.

Prepare to walk over dry ground

despite the swirl of wild wind,
the growl of rage,
the white capped lash of waves receding,
our footsteps, one by one,
will tread securely to liberation.

1632, Nicolas Poussin
National Gallery of Victoria, Melbourne

DIEGO FELIPE DE GUZMAN, MARQUIS OF LEGANES

Reveal only whatever I think is necessary:

the benign lineaments,
the fine apparel,
clothes that befit a wearer of distinction
and, behind the mask
unobserved by the eye that only sees outward appearances,
but perceived by an inner sense–

the lustrous empath quizzical to the gods,
understood by the divine,
in league with ancient wisdom–

the extraordinary heart
that beats with the foreknowledge of a seer,
the acumen in a brain saturated with melody

and,
in defiance of a pall covering the sea
and stifling the upsurge of gilded waves,
a thoroughly clear gaze
into the vigilance of the artist,
persuading him
not to covert the immaculate presence
before him,

but to render it truly
and commensurate with higher calling.

1634, Anthony van Dyck
The National Museum of Western Art, Tokyo

SAINT FRANCIS IN MEDITATION

Ecstasy
is shrouded by the passion of our Lord
who, terminally subdued by the excesses of the mob,
wept endless tears
for mothers contorted in childbirth,
the lame hunter stumbling on his own thong,
the gilded messenger torn from rightful entry,
and replaced by dumb excursus
into the fluid behind one's brow

prescience bounded by ice water
in eyes channeling the consequence
of birth in blood-stained rags,
the sublime touch
of an angel seeking a soft spot
in which to infuse rose scent high on the boughs

tainted by the skull's black regret,
contemplation of a foundling who,
in deference to the night blanketing the least inkling
of light,
would surrender to absence
tantalizingly close to complete otherness.

1635, Francisco de Zurbaran
National Gallery, London

LUCRETIA

The knife's perfect edge will cut purity
into my veins,
the sun's golden aura cleanse the blood flowing to my toes,
the warriors of virtue whiten my slumping body.

Unbroken skin will blot the heinous mark.

Swirling into the drunkenness of finality
will presuppose resurrection,
the blank stare auger tearlessness,
an inert breast,
the quiescent repose of a goddess's insight,
illuminate the shadows in bland hearts.

I will be vindicated.

1636, Guido Reni
The National Museum of Western Art, Tokyo

DUNE LANDSCAPE BY MOONLIGHT

What secrets do you reveal when the dark core is illuminated?

That you once,
when the pastor's back was turned,
pinched his purse
and spent the few pennies on cheap liquor

the woman you took
in the heat
of dirty passion was, indeed,
the wife of the local brewer

the cat you strangled,
leaving claw marks on your belly,
what, you said, was a struggle
with an opportunistic thief,
belonged to none other than your child

although
relieved of the burden weighing on you for years,
you would prefer, if you had your way,
the surreal glow painting its lonely brilliance
on every exposed surface
would be covered by a cloud,
the strange urge
to deliver unto another your meager confession
stay in the shadows,

and not lie

in the breast of another's potential

to light up your misdemeanors.

1636, Adriaen Brower

Gemäldegalerie, Berlin, Germany

HARBOR SCENE WITH LAMENTING HELIADES

In aching hearts,
tinctures of blue night
in aphrodisia well into our eyes,
unearthly pupils shift from scarlet water
to sap that fills a leaf
and fruit we'll drop
for solitary animals to devour.

Isolated in our grief,
we'll expect the breeze to caress our veins
in midair,
the soil to bind around our feet
and our midriff starting to harden
endure longer than we would in flesh and bone.

1640, Claude Lorraine
Wallraf-Richartz Museum, Cologne, Germany

VENUS AND ADONIS

For the slightest second eyes met,
hands brushed, and fingers entwined.

For the minutest of moments,
when the rain pattering in the snow
washed away their embrace,
the world stopped,
rhythm subsided,
and time crumpled.

For an instant
he paused and she wept.

"I am leaving you to seek my fortune
in the world,
leaving to commence my journey
to the unknown.
I am going where no man has been
or will follow,
leaving to corral the beast.

You have no claim on my destiny
I am free to travel on my own to the end

without your influence beguiling me to stay
at your side.

1640, Francesco Fanelli
Victoria and Albert Museum, London

NIGHT WATCH

We would be prepared to defend our city

at any cost
at the first sight of conflict,
gather as one,
prime our weapons,
discharge deadly pellets into the enemy's midst

consequent to incursion, form
into orderly ranks,
with one barrage of withering fire,
put an end
to the foe who would do us ill

for we are bound
to protect our loved ones,
preserve property rights

in the fog of war,
the calm days of peace,
never put to rest the inkling
that at any time
a menace could rise up from the darkness
and annihilate our light

maintain the stout resolution:

We will always be ready.

1642, Rembrandt
Rijksmuseum, Amsterdam

ITALIAN LANDSCAPE

Walking while listening
to every bird fill the air with song,
while stopping now and again
to taste liquid cool as evening

walking, protecting my shoulder
from the burns I receive,
taking note of ephemera
I could cast from my palette

walking, bound no more to empty platitudes
which keep me from reaching my haven,
unconstrained by lips
that ask for extra sugar in tea

walking, into the distance,
onward toward bright light
hovering above the horizon

conscious of belief disappearing, replaced
by certainty of matter becoming more
than can be conceived
through the eye of the senses

a perfect awakening:

expanse
of mind
embraced by the sun.

1645, Jan Both
Wallace Collection, London, England

CONFIRMATION

The awakening to the spirit in the breast,
the soul holding council with love,
the deeper longing to belong in the darkness
knowing the path to salvation

the balancing of mind
with the entreating of the heart
to trust the purity of silence,
the compassion to enter another soul
and hear its striving for light

the trial to secure a place
in the bosom of sanctified being
evidenced at the foot of the Master
who has accomplished the trial.

1645, Nicolas Poussin
Scottish National Gallery, Edinburgh, Scotland

TOILET OF VENUS

With a touch of light on my cheek,
I'll chase the shadow
into the darkness

a dab of powder on my lashes,
flutter like a butterfly
to and fro toward the moon

rouge on my lips,
taste the sweetest flow
from bramble to rose,
to aphrodisia returning to my palate

and then,
comely as the wind caressing the surface
of blue lakes,
ice melting under the touch
of a gentle finger,
the opening sunflower
to the day's rotation,
I'll await a suitor,
who, no doubt,
will never resist the moist wish

to surrender unto the poignancy
of my heartbeat.

1647, Diego Velazquez
National Gallery, London

PASTORAL WITH THE ARCH OF CONSTANTINE

Fallen out with maudlin, wide-open mouths
tranquilized
by acrid blood
and traumatized by fear of falling,
disavowing entry from nether regions
in tow of babelic need
to shatter the one true vision,
I'll keep my distance

the hills blue,
the sky reaching into absence,
the misty town alluring with promise
of warm flame,
cirrus tresses,
and clean white
approachable by an hour on foot

no bells tolling out the end,
no whispers condemning a pauper's cessation,
no maleficent glances
at sores and wounded feet

pollen dust rising with the breeze
and settling on yellow petals,
the cow's low mooing suggesting contentment

with warm shade
and undulating pasture

the triumphant arch opening inner space
for a procession through murmuring ease,
the young man,
pronouncing each syllable with relish,
reciting an ode gifted from the denizens
of ancient climes:

abundant
in rest,
clement in drowsy afternoon speech,
settling into the sleep of rose dew
and wine,
we'll share each drop.

1648, Claude Lorraine
Kunsthaus, Zurich, Switzerland

THE EMBARKATION OF THE QUEEN OF SHEBA

Hope I will withstand the savage sea.

Fret not, madam of royal blood,
the sublime touch upon the waves
enough to assure us
you will reach your destination unscathed,
the study men who ply their way across the water
inspire us
to believe you will arrive safely,
the stout rigging strong as spider's web,
although imbued with the softest light,
will hold together any structure
that deigns to leave the security
found in the abeyance of tempest
realized for all life.

Pray for my return.

Allay your fear, my lady.
the late afternoon glows' a premonition
of a gladsome heart

your hands in His revealing the nexus
between yellow sand
and fertile winds,

ancient rock
and warm saltwater lapping the shore

willingness to cede sovereignty
to the blessing you will incur.

1648, Claude Lorraine
National Gallery, London

VIEW OF LA CRESCENZA

Buried here amongst the trees,
decaying,
I could breathe in the aroma of petals,
light, and verdure

sandwiched amongst ripe summer days,
dying with the leaves,
I could taste ambrosia

enclosed in the stains upon a twisted stump,
arriving with significance from eternity,
I'll seek a memory harder to find
than delight in the sublime heart
which calls home
the nexus with sanity:

once free to roam.

1649, Claude Lorraine
Metropolitan Museum, New York

A MAN IN ARMOR

In untilled fields crisscrossing a nightmare,
gently shivering in unerotic colors
transferred through the question,
How can I do it?
How? to lush folds of woven cloth,
the fervent warrior who,
in ethereal garb betraying a less than pure heart,
aims to end tyranny
by the thrust into the core
that expands only at the expense
of similarly endowed,
semi-conscious entities demanding hegemony over all existence

when the Lamb's moist dignity
is raised into the spleen venting fury,
forgoes the severe clash of steel
upon steel, salt stale stains,
and a bone protruding entrails

each time forgiveness and mercy
is uttered as the way of all
who seek greatness of spirit,
retreat toward the mist swirled,
tri crossed hill guarding the principle of life,
resurrection,
and the word becoming the master
enclosing us like lost sheep under the vault of truth.

Brother you shall remain
my sword.
In the tomb's unstirred odor
we shall long no more for glory

1655, Rembrandt
City Art Gallery, Glasgow, Scotland

FRANCISCAN FRIAR

Lucid touch
benign as flecks of snow onto an eye,
idyllic slumber
warm as spring wind bringing pollen
to bear upon a solitary stem,
translucent echoes
decipherable
as the first word uttered
to naked flesh reposing in twilight,
homely shadows dense
as mountain's lee before the break of dawn

bone and flesh
vacant as the memory
of the miller's daughter,
the rush of white water under the wheel,
and what it took to deny life.

1655, Rembrandt
National Gallery, London

WOODED HILLSIDE WITH A VIEW OF BENTHEIM CASTLE

Give me a reason
why I should concentrate
on the sun burning sharp detail under every lid,
and leaving dazzlement on the path
to the heights?

That because we can see our way clearly,
the ghouls lurking in the shadows
will be countered
before they rout our senses,
eviscerate good intentions
and leave us exhausted?

So, surprising it may seem,
I still want to delve
an inch above the netherworld,
transfix my gaze on the mountain's lee
where the water is always cold
and the gelid film
under a leaf sets until the vein dies,
turn inwards from the rose
and feel the thorn's prick in my side

for breath arises far from the surface,
life springs from the depths no one can view,
momentum,

at its very beginning,
silent
as air caught in the sheltered night,
leaps unannounced into a black frame.

1655, Jacob van Ruisdael
Art Gallery of New South Wales, Sydney

A LADY WITH A PINK

They motioned toward the brimming sea,
and I refreshed in the early morning hue.

They told me he would return,
and I found life
in borrowing scent from the folds.

The years sagged under the weight
of condolence
and inward turning lips,
and I drew breath
under gentle hands

which will bury me alone.

1660, Rembrandt
Metropolitan Museum, New York

WINTER (THE FLOOD)

Nothing
can prepare us for the downpour

it flows from outside our will,
drowns entreaty for supplication,
enters every nook and crevice
with the intention of obliterating sensibility.

It is folly
to assume we have the capacity
to stem the flow.

It enters from God forsaken darkness
with a rush of blind passion,
annihilates the one true door
we could open onto clemency,
subjugates the growing plant
within our bones

to a fathomless depth,
obfuscating our sight into the clear sky
blue as lapis lazuli,
plunges our sensitivity into dark grey.

To where
will we swim if we say afloat?

To the edge,
thirsty for an arid plain,
fall over

to the glistening rocks, lose our foothold,
fall back into the abyss

with supreme effort, to the horizon

hope,
at last
the lightning will hit us

deliver us out of misery.

1660, Nicolas Poussin
Louvre, Paris, France

WOMAN WITH A PEARL NECKLACE

She's not your ordinary, bored mistress
burdened with the untoward expectations
of her kind.

No, she's a whisper of ineffable grace
who,
transported from the star in velvet night,
shines before the glow
that returns and brightens each fleck
and shadow on her smooth countenance.

She's not a dowdy servant who must answer the call
of a master determined to overflow her status.

No, she's a moon blessed sweetheart
who has lost a lover
and, airily poised on the verge
of beauty seeking Aphrodite,
the serene goddess who,
at every moment through the doorway
between enchantment
and the flickering wings of angels passing eyelids,
can expect the suitor uplifting a cache
of scintillating thread

to appear
at her footstool.

1662, Johannes Vermeer
Gemäldegalerie, Berlin

SELF PORTRAIT 63 YEARS

Oh lord,
I have suffered your touch,
and have settled into dying streams

laden with the derisive languor
which characterizes life
and the ignoble gesture
I have undertaken to reach thee.

1670, Rembrandt
National Gallery, London

CHARLES II

I am quick witted.
I have perfect, stately grace
brought forth by my breeding,
a long line of accomplished nobility
having no flaws or temperament
unsuited to leading a country
through tempestuous conditions.

Above all,
I value my access to spiritual clarity
brought out of the mystification
of the ages to my presence,
so with it
I can address all kind of being
how to live in accordance
with the beauty and power of honorable light.

I am certain I have found a greatness within,
which can bear the might thrown against this state
from forces
whose purpose
it is to dominate
and control our life.

I can readily arm us
to triumph over adversity.

How dare you neglect your duty
to listen to my commandments,
as they are received from the highest, purest
most illustrious power there can be.

You dare to mock such grace.

You will be executed.

All manner
of being will fall at my bidding,
all belief will revel in my way.

I will rule.
I am the architect of universal meaning

can accept no other as my sovereign.

1678, John Bushnell
Fitzwilliam Museum, Cambridge, England

ASCANIUS SHOOTING THE STAG OF SYLVIA

A fleeting glimpse between the trees—

terror in the heroic chamber,
dynamically marking the beast.

A spirit whetting the will
to remain listening to a calling
to put an end
to the slaughter.

A gust of wind opening the clouds—

a hallowed space
to protect the animal
before he spikes the body,

A wilderness
in which to fly through the forest unchecked
into the distant,
ever receding future.

A voice to reveal the danger
of taking from the earth
harmonious balance—

speed and dainty movement.

The ability
to leap beyond cruelty into the distance
of my dream—

tantamount to supernal light,
a brush exceeding the moment
of its inception.

Transmutation of desire
into a haven—

the witness
to whitewashed clouds building further into nothingness

My life's ambition—

mythical abundance preventing the murderous folly.

1682, Claude Lorraine
Ashmolean Museum, Oxford, England

LANDSCAPE IN THE STYLE OF HUANG GONGWANG

The brief instance,
the positive, the vain,
realization and strength
will evaporate someday
when I surrender my sovereignty
and comfort
in the bosom of nature

the shift from dead wood compacted in a crevice
to the dry wind circulating a mass
of leaves,
luminous peaks aware of their own distance
from a penetrating eye
to the abode
that could be mine,
if, for a moment of forgetfulness,
I dropped my brush into the dirty stream

earth's tender shoots breaking into shade
beneath a twisted pine
to the bright rays,
now there, now absent,
forming one, blank glare on my forehead.

1687, Wang Yanqui
Hayward Gallery, London

THE AVENUE AT MIDDELHARNIS

On the other side of the horizon,
another viewer looks toward the disappearing point
he vainly tries to perceive
as I do

his helplessness melts into mine,
my inadequacy meets his

streaming back from the center,
void
as timelessness,
inert with fruitlessness,
the empty origin
formless
as a nought
perfectly poises to open

our confluence transcending the one only.

1689, Meindert Hobbema
National Gallery, London

BUDDHA

Cloud light in your eyes,
a mountain in your spine.

What illusions are left?

Will they disappear
like the cherry blossoms,
or remain
like the mist over Mt Fuji.

1690, Statue
Tennoji Temple, Yanaka, Tokyo, Japan

# 18th Century

WHITE MAGNOLIA, HEMP PALM AND BANANA PLANTS

The white magnolia easily bruised,
the banana plant easily torn,
the hemp
easily crushed

the observer,
tending to every fragile detail,
easily rendered superfluous.

1700s, Attributed to Tatebayashi Kagei
The Nezu Museum, Tokyo

VENUS DISARMING CUPID

I'm afraid, so afraid
of serpents crawling between my ribs,
of tendrils creeping inexorably
toward my throat
and lodging behind my eyes.

Could you have sheaved your weapon?

My limbs long for his fiery thrust,
cheeks burn with blood,
my void clamors to be filled with his scent.

Did you drop
from the clouds with intent,
or was it a foolish lapse
of concentration that penetrated my breast?

The swirling wind numbs the sense
above my brow,
the flight of herons brings a downdraft
of warm air on my neck,
the tide rises through my calves.

How could you be so remiss?

I'll take your bow and arrow
and with my newly found surge of passion
tear them to splinters.

1700–10, Corneille van Cleve
National Museum of Western Art, Tokyo

IRISES

So blue, the sky divorced of air
congeals in a clump,
until one form from another
barely holds apart
by a shade softer than its origin

eternity distills far ends
in liquid soaking tissue,
midnight perceived though an open window
stains a furl

so green,
life expanding toward the sun concentrates in a vein,
the force articulating the height
and depth of endeavor
severs with the curve of each leaf

the burst
of momentum contained in a tip

so natural,
an iris propagates in my heart
and drenches each beat,
represses its own will
to flourish in deep soil,
grows without submission

through my tendons
and brush.

1701–5, Ogata Korin
Nezu Museum, Tokyo

FRANCOIS ARMAND DI GOUTANT

Betwixt bellicosity and submission—
the capacity to retreat
or advance
as circumstances dictate,
merging with the mob
or standing aloof,
inflated with superior aura—
able to raise a glass with the lowliest
yet, as darkness precedes the dawn
of earnest conflict,
open to the text that enlightens flesh
and inspires the limbs
to stand at the head of a multitude.

But in this case?

A stupid man with power is dangerous.

A great mistake would be not to lie
before the face of desuetude
and turn my back on the glazed eye
that will see its formation as the perfect orb
round as the moon
and, ensconced
as a rose in early morning blush,
its princely demeanor as the poetaster's liberation
from dead ended verse

a warrior determined
to invite deities into his ardor,
cross swords with an angel,
and elope to Mars with a horde in trail.

1714, Nicolas de largilliere
Museum of Fine Arts, Boston, Massachusetts

THE DANCE

Enchanted with the humorous glance
of a goddess
on the denizens below,
surrender until Spring touches lips,
and play and sing and poetize.

Butterfly,
through mist and Heaven shining,
touch the moon's round glow
poise feet perfectly on an updraft of warm air,
descend on a leaf
and wait for the breeze to ruffle wings.

Princess,
in the midst
of mild aether forewarning lassitude
and impoverishment,
anticipate your first delicate step

with the silent frost
of slumber,
echo from eternity's whisper,
dance
until the leaves tremble,
the stars divulge night's gleam

white blossom powder
defenseless
as a shadow chased by the sun at noon.

1719, Antoine Watteau
Gemäldegalerie, Berlin

PENGLAI, ISLAND OF THE IMMORTALS

Eat heat shed from the sun,
dance
on pools reflecting the visage
of predecessors
who stare as if they'll belong with us

but,
after a moment suspended in ice,
will notice the difference
in eyelids touching the flesh
of new arrivals,
who longed to catch up
with a thousand years preceding the ones
who look down upon us

swallow the fire,
with feet contained in a glow,
reach the one
who was born yesterday,
who'll die before his ancestor,
and corroded as the hill,
stout as the pine,
count another inch
of wood tomorrow.

1723, Yuan Jiang
Hayward Gallery, London

FLOWERS IN A VASE

Change of heart:

Empowered to amend the rotting core,
surpass the shadow congealed
in dogma,
realize compassion with the natural scene:

a daub emanates from harmony,
every note echoes a symphony
of leaf, calyx, and stem:

a chrysanthemum likened to a mother's heart,
a butterfly's wing to her dance without cessation

the tendril entering azure scented
with rose to reaching out of embitterment,
bloodletting washed into the river
and into the sea
to the delicate face smearing apricot China

a sunburst to the carnation,
the vein in agony to the violet.

1726, Jan van Huysum,
Wallace Collection, London

SLEEPING SHEPHERDESS

I'll blame Venus
incumbent in clouds for my folly.
Just one kiss
and I'll trip lightheartedly away.
Should she awaken, I'll forfeit good grace
and beg her to believe
that her mystique
was so compelling I had no choice

I blundered into rapture,
threw off all pretense
of decorum

planted my lips on hers.

1730, Nicolas Lancret
The National Museum of Western Art, Tokyo

THE SCHOOL MISTRESS

With dedication,
willing to trust the issue from her heart,
willing to lead him further into the light,
longing to see a vision changing sorrow,
and invalidating it?

A test to grow unhindered,
a challenge to maintain a goal,
a trial to relinquish the wiles,
which she will evict
at the behest of the Master,
inspiring him to prepare for a journey
of greater importance?

Embedded in her breast and soul
the source of wonder,
security, contentment, purity,
and protection from malignant expectations
severing reason into frittered exoduses,
she'll avoid?

And with caring,
willing to substitute her finer feeling
for the coarse, brutal sense
she'll endeavor to discover
at the heart of the baby,
and change it?

No! Persecuting him,
willing him forward to create plans,
ambition, and destiny,
forward to triumph over nature,
onward,
utilizing his excellence
to control the very carriage he inhabits
with his power.

And, invoking the precedent of centuries old tradition,
neglecting the desire of the child
to seek his delight and peace,
instilling a set of rules within the mind,
within the body
which likes to feel the way forward.

1737, Jean Simeon Chardin
National Gallery, London

HANDEL

Here,
there are no words to articulate the founding
of higher empires near to the summit
we'd climb if our limbs were sturdy,
the rarefied air breathed easily,
only the strum
of the lyre echoing the virgin's relief
in freedom from enslavement,
no discourse elevating ideals
to the plane
where Osiris tended to an open flower
and Isis, gaudily attired,
burst forth in scent
and powder,
only the downward stroke vivifying the fall
of an extraterrestrial visitant
into the somber arms
of a mother fully prepared to cradle light
on the verge of deliverance from a meaner glow

no mindful utterance
to tell how Jupiter and Mars
cross each other's paths at midnight,
only the barely discernable thrum
in an attentive ear
ready to receive the confluence
of dynasties conveying one life span,

Scripture plunging the depths
of misery
and rising to apotheosis,
the deities seeking a channel
to divulge an earnest wish for perpetuity

one human heart redirecting their wish
to another ear
distant from the source
as the furthest planet from the sun

1738, Louis-Francois Roubiliac
Victoria and Albert Museum, London

THE PIAZZA SAN MARCO

Graze my knuckles
on stone,
allow the blood to seep
into mortar,
challenge my breath to form clouds,
the marrow
in my bones to color the steps

trust my eye to glance from the same height
as a visitor surveying each plume
and bouquet below,
an angle
from my joints,
sharp as the edge between yesterday
and a day ago,
define every relation
between square,
building, and cloud.

I could grasp a coattail,
converse with a peasant,
approach a Lord
with full realization:

I belong
in the midst of life
in Venice.

1742–46, Canaletto
Art Gallery of New South Wales, Sydney

THE BANQUET OF CLEOPATRA

A ghost bleeds into nacre
and leaves a drop from its heart,
a pearl dissolves in wine
and steeps the odor of ocean
in the grape,
the mixture settles near the spine
and rises in the moon

our vanity pickled egg,
our hubris rich as broiled loin,
our indulgence deep
as a pitcher of oil.

You'll cross to a land of verdure
and rain,
I'll subsist in hot winds
and sand

you'll taste the sweat of a lover,
my palate will dry with age

our tryst will endure
like steam on hot iron.

1743–44, Giambattista Tiepolo
National Gallery of Victoria, Melbourne

THE PAINTER AND HIS PUG

If I had three wishes–

to unearth primal water
and allow it to refresh each stroke,
caress the stars
and bring the light back into the canvas,
instantiate the sublimest Ideal
and suffuse each hue
with translucence–

I'd alter all of them

for even if the tempest
were to subside in my heart,
I know not how
to transfer the image
onto the squalor and filth I detest.

1745, William Hogarth
Tate Gallery, London

THE MYSTERIOUS BASKET

A grove where nymphs
and shadows intermingle,
the air drowsy
and numbed
with the hum
of golden bees.

She slumbers in their faraway presence.

A cochineal sunset faded
on the backs of satyrs
who,
enamored with dew and rose water,
sought bedraggled figures to lie upon.

He places a bouquet
in reach
of her intimate senses.

Dynasties crumbled,
the moon lit up statues strewn between rocks,
shards of earthenware
formed patterns no one could piece together.

She'll press each flower
against her breast
on awakening.

1748, Francois Boucher
National Gallery of Victoria, Melbourne

PORTRAIT OF AN OLD WOMAN

The flame died years ago,
now only an ember

an undaunted eye receding from my gaze,
a faint glimmer on a forest pool

water springing and emptying into a lover's heart,
a stilling stream finding no outlet
but the trickle in a deceased heart.

The days run into the same from yesteryear,
the patterns in my face deepen
with the moon's cycle ever more distant

twilight encountered before midnight frost
provides a foretaste of earth's purblind encirclement.

Today, I have cleared my shelves
of mementoes, leaving only one:

the shoe my son wore to his christening

tiny as the sparrow at the window.

1749–50, Christian Seybold
Harvard Art Museums, Cambridge, Massachusetts

PORTRAIT GROUP: THE SINGER FARINELLI AND FRIENDS

Night
has no shadow
that can't be uplifted with a breath
of light,
midday no glare
that can't be softened with dulcet tones

the ocean won't penetrate a teardrop,
the mountain won't dominate a hillock

the tempestuous sea calmed with a steady note,
the curl
of a wave reduced with a lilt from moist throats

and,
as silence threatens to numb ears
and quietude dull the heart
with pallor,
our voices will raise
to the sun

and sing.

1750–52, Jacopo Amigoni
National Gallery of Victoria, Melbourne

POETESS ONO NO KOMACHI

Spirit,
did you catch the manner
in which she prayed?
Drawn to the sun by heat—
a lark,
dulcet mistress born on the horizon
between ice and light.
Did you watch her glide over a glossy surface,
sweeping debris from her path,
eliciting every vowel
with rounded fingers,
every syllable with a quick turn,
every word that means health
with a short step

dancing in decency.

1762, Harunobu
British Museum, London

SELF PORTRAIT

My aroma
is of aphrodisia melting in candlelight,
the lingering air known to Venus
stilling my fingers
before the first dab evokes the lucence
she'd have worn
in her brush with human folly.

My brow means the same to your wise,
inward turning gaze,
as the initial glance on features
that could,
if the Muse imbued soft hands
with the flow and stillness embodying her own,
draw a Euboean hunter
toward the glint in an eye

in the centuries to come,
hold the longing
of a suitor,
if only
in swirls
and touches of paint.

1763, Marie-Gabrielle Capet
The National Museum of Western Art, Tokyo

LANDSCAPE WITH SHEPHERDS AND FLOCK OF SHEEP

Tales of invincible might
have little value in the hollow
where shepherds gather and rest.
A cup
of warm tea and a nod toward the flock
elicits a murmur known to their forebears
who, too, gladly received similar rumination
from the earth
and evening quietude:

watch the leader,
make sure her head nestles in your lap,
smell the air
for scent tasting of bristling hair,
hot breath, and wild need

keep one lid open and one lid closed:

firelight dancing on black eyes,
blood drawing toward a sinking head,
night staining cloud light,
forest shadows matching the silence
in a heart.

1763, Jean-Honore Fragonard
The National Museum of Western Art, Tokyo

MISS SUSANNAH GALE

Calm my joy
in the daubs and splashes
on white canvas.

Despite the protection
of wealth and status, the arch nemesis
known as penury will clasp at your ankles,
the plight
of the many filter though the lace
in your gown.

Diminish my aspiration
to bestow largesse
with felicity
and perspicacity.

The corroded,
the exhausted, the pitiful
are always on the lookout
for succor

their drift from the well spring
a constant drain on the source.

Temper my desire
to live unfettered through the tempest.

The wilting rose, the dry stem,
the thorn's sharp edge
presage the distant pall descending on the earth
before the blinds shut at sunset.

Cause my beauty
to lose its eternal bloom.

That,
as God is my witness,
I can never do.

1763–64, Sir Joshua Reynolds
National Gallery of Victoria, Melbourne

FLOATING ANGEL

Air so light the birds cannot rise,
a beat so fine a heart cannot resonate,
a touch so gentle
the moon cannot feel

a message a ready ear *can* perceive:

silence
in the treetops,
a trance in the boughs,
immanence in the outer edges

the gate open.

1770, Ignaz Gunther
Germanisches Nationalmuseum, Nuremberg, Germany

SEAPORT BY MOONLIGHT

Under no coercion
to face what lurks behind the wall
of immanence–

a pure womb preparing for delivery,
a child supping blood spilt into its hand–

a sensitivity in the heart reminds me
to surrender longing to partake solely
in reason,
to believe only things proffering salvation,
to hold vainly
to the outside
unable to divulge secrecy

a seeker,
who'll wait
for the return of a word
to guide him back
into the womb
of darkest night.

1771, Joseph Vernet
Louvre, Paris

VIEW OF THE VENETIAN LAGOON WITH THE TOWER OF MALGHERA

Divide light from shadow
and empty the rainbow in between,
search the edges
for absence
and fill the center
with life,
delve into the middle and taste the salt,
but leave a bland taste
where the borders fall into nothingness

when conscience enlightens an invidious retreat,
come close
to the bodies and feel their heat

dissolve silence
into activity
and feel the hues scattering saturation,
reconfigure bones with chalk
and let mountain water mingle in brine

divorce hardness
from the ephemeral,
the shallow from the depths,
set the surface to face the sun

for the while humanity impinges on my nerves,
stand on the opposite shore.

C 1770, Francesco Guardi
National Gallery, London

THE HOUSE OF CARDS

I can remark on dexterity:

one card
after another–

a breath–

not too long

quickly for Christendom
upheld by an act
of inerrant judgement–

a pause–
gently
to stop catastrophe,
another
as if times drive
to secure a place
beyond imprisonment
has abated

hence,
to look to a structure a king could desire.

I can sense your expectation:

the margin between success and failure
is measured
by the precise placement, with foresight,
of each individual component making up the totality
known as your own accomplishment.

I can see what you are trying to achieve:

you are erecting an edifice,
a house of cards,
to cushion you
from the knocking in
of the limitations you cannot perceive.

1775, Jean-Simeon Chardin
National Gallery, London

DIANA AND HER NYMPHS BATHING

Will my voice float through the penumbra
of solitude,
the water swirled
by my toe flow to your ears,
cleansing them to amplitude?
A flaxen curl douched in Spring,
a breast bland as day drenched in wet,
a round eye sodden in a rill.

Is our beauty perceivable?

Tender parts lathed in an odorless pool,
fingers dripping drops that splash upon rocks,
heels touching ground
free of pebbles.

Will our delight
ever filter to your senses?

A stain that could be a bruise
whitened
in an instant,
a tear under a lid
submerged in a whirl

when we swim,
the ache in a rib,

hardly apparent to an outflying dove,
blanched
in silence

the ecstasy
of need to dry when we emerge
held off somewhat
by the coolness rushing through our veins.

Am I through to you yet?

1778–82, Angelica Kauffman
Art Gallery of South Australia, Adelaide

THE LISTENING GIRL

Imminent,
the day's turn toward sunset

pristine,
the night's burden lifted by moonlight

barely noted,
as if tomorrow were blind

beyond the grave,
effortlessly instantiated

the call!

1780, Jean-Baptiste Greuze
Wallace Collection, London

SELF PORTRAIT IN A STRAW HAT

Servitor of mystical happenstance,
refresh the confluence of wisdom and ordinary,
everyday patter.

Muse of the beautiful,
gel light,
flourish,
and the imprint from natural creation
in the curves
and stresses under my hand.

Eminent daughter
of time's slow progress,
receive the weight
of Art's unraveling in the brushes
of forebears

and, coaxing my deft skills
into the reflection I perceive
of what I could be,
channel your sustenance through my veins,
your insight through my eyes

your delicate touch through my fingers.

1782, Élisabeth Loise Vigée Le Brun
National Gallery, London

THE DEATH OF MAJOR PIERSON

Veins rupture, my son

pipes burst in sallow lips,
the tune transfigures into paste.

An offensive death, my Lord.

Hewn from creation
and damned to destroy men
who obey no other than love,
darkness colludes with Hell,
skulls leer inwards,
doves futter upwards,
rain drops back to Heaven

and I sleep,
till dawn tired and wan,
regains possession of life.

1783, John singleton Copley
Tate Gallery, London

THEODORE MEETS IN THE WOOD THE SPECTER OF HIS ANCESTOR GUIDO CAVALCANTI

Mad eyes that envisage a body
immobile in fear,
muscle and brawn evaporating in nebula

crazed eyes that long to pierce white meat,
the beat of a heart
in demise,
inner tissue quartered with a blade

baby blue eyes that entertain a claw,
drown in blood,
float disembodied
until popping on the surface

semi-conscious eyes
entrapped
in sangfroid,
gorged
with blindness turning purblind,
that,
on the cusp of nihil assuming a face,
perceive the eyes

that closed
when suicide sliced through gel.

1783, Johann Fuseli
The National Museum of Western Art, Tokyo

MR AND MRS WILLIAM HALLETT ('THE MORNING WALK')

I'll catch a robin
and persuade it to sing

grass exudes the odor of fresh milk,
sycamore seeds dream of flutter
and twirl,
dandelion fluff loosens from a stem

a wish:

I hope the dew won't drench our shoes.

I'll blow a kiss
toward the ruins
where our forefathers lie

leaves shift in the breeze,
sunlight dapples a bole,
bubbles pop on the lake

a promise:

I'll follow
till the oak wood fails to sprout.

I'll stake my life on faithfulness

shadows flit between stone and weeds,
a ray brightens a clearing,
scintilla burn like coals
in your eyes

a surety:

after the years
I'll hold your hand despite its frailty.

I'll approach the gate
with the intention
of crossing with you

clouds cover the glare,
a sparrow descends in a thicket,
roots taste the spring
the truth:

our descendants
will chance upon this path as we have.

1785, Thomas Gainsborough
National Gallery, London

THE DEATH OF SOCRATES

I have no Master
to whom I must submit,
no ethereal voice transfiguring the catchment
in my breast,
no mercurial spirit messaging the cosmos:

"We rule,
we expect obedience

we build the clouds, evoke thunder

in voluptuous swirls countermanding the descent
into your bones,
rise again
into a dream magnifying red birds
and golden claws."

Give me the bitter juice
and numbness
will creep from my feet to my heart.

Exonerated from the trial of the ignorant,
free of the intoxication
the deities
of the multitude would melt into prescience,

I'll evade the ticks
and flies crawling on my eyes.

1787, Jacques-Louis David
Metropolitan Museum, New York

ITALIAN LANDSCAPE WITH BATHERS

Our skin receives the pool's nourishment

rubicund drones pursed the heady queen,
ova fused pallor and need.

The drops on our skin reflect paradise

ghostly internment diminished at our heels,
refulgent climes sweltered
in veins of blue in orange.

Amorous glances illuminate an idyll

nakedness, forthwith,
will blind the errant,
pink lips breathe the flow from Orion

in surreptitious winds losing heat
through dalliance,
the maudlin guardian,
now divested of his rule,
will allow the warmth in our breasts
to loosen the dew a pauper sips.

1790, Pierre Henri de Valenciennes
Museum of Fine Art, Boston, Massachusetts

THE LOVERS, CHUBEI AND UMEGAWA

I'll protect you from the wind,
the snow, the ice,
the hail

until you retreat from my caress.

I'll surrender to the iron glance,
the pursed lips,
the glint in your eye

until you abuse my longing
with compliments thrown from waywardness
and nonchalance.

I'll adorn your figure with dream spun curtains
swathing barely visible
around your breasts

until you lie about the fruit you stole.

I'll treasure the courtesan's dance
I'll enact,
entranced by an emperor's gaze
following every step

until you fall asleep.

We'll promise to stop bickering,
place our own wishes after the others,
never to repeat folly

until the day after next.

1797, Kitagawa Utamaro
British Museum, London

A SCENE FROM 'THE FORCIBLY BEWITCHED'

Bright, bright light, shine in my eyes,
flicker in my brain, inflame my heart

keep the ghouls at bay,
the insects from crawling on my spine,
the darkness from creeping to the roof

forever, I shall reaffirm your presence

anon, renew your glow

in this instance,
feed your refulgence

your brilliance shall sustain me,
your white center enamor my blood,
your heat invigorate breath rising
and depleting with every cold gust

stay alive, my sweet

linger in perpetuity, my beauty

burn within me.

1798, Francisco de Goya
National Gallery, London

19th Century

NAPOLEON AS MARS THE PEACEMAKER

What you assume:

the call to realize the hope
of millions, limitless pressing, weightlessness
of love

forbearance entangling the thread holding sentimentality
to perfection,
farsightedness in the face
of all
who would misuse you

a winged cherub guiding you
to utmost glory and mastery beyond night

scarlet tissue opening to the birth
of a martyr,
defiant mortal prizing toenails from grit
and splicing limbs with aether?

1802 (1811), Antonio Canova
Palazzo Brera, Milan, Italy

THESEUS AND THE CENTAUR

Your breath smells of rotten hay
and maiden's eyes

pores clogged with mucus,
dream of blood red flanks
and ripened skulls.

Surrender, surrender

or I'll strike and dash you to pieces.

The moon translates a feeble glow
into radiance,
a sparrow descends into a nest
and pecks at its young

the voice of temerity bursts into my ears.

Kill him!

1806, Antonio Canova
Kunsthistorisches Museum, Vienna

WILLIAM BLAKE

Exhuming into the sphere
lowliness cannot pursue,
vigilance extricates from rounded shoulders
and cleft palates,
prismatic colors bend toward the center
of your brow.

Anointed soul,
blessed in following He
who stood amongst us,
raised and inclining toward an open ear.

Words tumble from paradisal chords,
lines and fractured circles
assume the guise of creator
and created,
fire pelts like rain,
statues contort into life,
serenity pops in ardor
and milliseconds lengthen
into a day upon a century.

Priest of the unknown seems foreign to us,
as if we didn't exist.

Where are you?

1807, Thomas Phillips
National Portrait Gallery, London

GOETHE

Does color stain aether,
illuminate perfumed clouds, settle
in your bones
and contrast numinous night with the cumuli of desire?

Have I heard you speak to me?
Do you know the way my friend?

Amiable as a waif rescued from depravity,
translucent
as the peak in sight of a god,
does an answer resonate with Plato's leap
from the cave,
permeate your fore lobe?

Or are you beyond me
inebriated with questions?

1810, Gerhard von Kügelen
Goethe Museum, Düsseldorf, Germany

WINTER LANDSCAPE

Vials of honey, flaxen locks,
the pitter-patter splurge of tears
compassionate on my brow
can dissolve in the mist.

Rather,
one spike from my ribs to my toes.

Hymns, hands weaving toward the numinous breach
between numbness and ecstasy,
crowded lineaments paling before the pulpit's rage,
can freeze in tombs below a white blanket.

Rather, a steady clomp on bold feet
leaving an imprint six inches deep.

Not bells pealing hope of interminable cessation
from winter's deathly hush,
the refrain beckoning incarnate gentleness
to blend with each act of nurturing the child,
or wisdom leading a wayfarer
though the drifts blinding progress

but, in my case, submitting my plea,
merely a rigid spine holding the weight
of my head.

1811, Caspar David Friedrich
National Gallery, London

TRUTH HAS DIED

Plate 79 from The Disasters of War

Break my back
and place me on a pyre,
linger over my white breast
until flames curl around my bosom,
gather my ash
and sprinkle it on your foreheads

the mark will wash off in a flow of tears,
the tears congeal in sweat
and drip to your knees,
your knees buckle in the weight
of my absence.

Who will hold your child
when it bleeds,
scour the grit under your fingernails,
settle the lion's breath in a lunge?

The morning will break
with the same pallid cast,
blackbirds warble with strangled tones,
nightshade open in pungent fumes

in the cloisters a heavy sigh
will meet an eye turning toward the wall:

"The roast will be fine sprinkled with thyme."

1814–15, Francisco Goya
The National Museum of Western Art, Tokyo

THE MUTINY ON THE RAFT OF THE MEDUSA

Forgo tenderness
you felt as a child,
rake logic over the coals,
scuttle worship and prayer

nothing, absolutely nothing
can make sense of crazed depths
and nothing offers no comfort either.

Placate welling blood
with salt water,
reduce savagery with damp clouds,
annihilate rising bile with a splinter

out of the reaches
of calm,
goat's heads and lamb's tongues bleat
with gusto:

"We know
we have the answer
if we look into the fetid mess
of severed limbs,
will find enlightenment
if we gaze long enough
into bloated eyes and cadaverous skin

with putrid jaws,
echo the cries
in a godforsaken night

echo the meaning of inhumanity."

1818, Théodore Géricault
Fogg Art Museum, Cambridge, Massachusetts

MEDITATING FROG

Cold blood,
an ancient croak and green legs.
What more could a froggy think about?

Moonlight,
flies and a ripple.
What other gifts
could satisfy a dreamer on a lily pad?

Midnight silence, the pond's overflow
and spawn clogging the reeds.
What else can the future expect
from one of his kind?

1820s, Sengai Gibon
Idemitsu Museum of Arts, Tokyo

HAY WAIN

Grief won't stain the edges
nor calumny char the core

with age old,
never to be distanced from the languor
of summer's height,
the turning wheel from rose lit mornings
until the flare of evening
will erase the voices clamoring
to undo the bond between moisture above,
water below,
and the sweat on a brow in between.

Friction won't disquiet the nexus
between man, beast and shadow
nor irreverence mar the infusion
of silence into a rumble
and shuffling stalks

timeless as a cathedral's nave perpetuating song,
clear as the oration
of a committed parson,
the eternal rising in the fluctuations
and flecks making up the whole
will barely be noticed
by a passerby
in haste to reach his next appointment.

Erudition won't cloud the senses
nor virtuosity blind perception
with a calling from ancient climes

buckets full will still be gathered,
clouds build inexorably until dissipation,
and divorced from features resembling the haunt
of an Euboean mistress,
a humble abode provide respite
from cruel winds veering from the north.

1821, John Constable
National Gallery, London

SALISBURY CATHEDRAL FROM THE BISHOP'S GROUNDS

Let me live freely from sorrow
alongside you
in ecstasy

missed chance, like wind passed?

An avid call highlighted:
Trust me",
echo, "
Trust me."

Vision
of altitude,
white spire bearing rain,
willing gusts
of passion away from me.

1823, John Constable
Victoria and Albert Museum, London

OLD BEECH TREE

There is sap in my veins,
bark on my shins,
rings around my heart.
I smell of old wood
dank
as mold,
taste droplets
bloodless as a cold night,
breathe in the green
of innumerable leaves
dense as the thicket sprouting virgin growth.

My arm is broken,
my back stunted,
my bole blanched
with the rout of winter upon spring.

I will survive
until felled by an axe,
an unlikely fire chars my innards

or,
with the confluence
of lightning and broken earth,

I crack open
and lie roots upended.

1828–30, Camille Corot
Museum of Fine Arts, Boston, Massachusetts

GREAT WAVE OFF THE COAST OF KANAGAWA

It could crash though Fuji and swallow the moon,
drench our eyes
and saturate thick boards with salt.

The mountain becomes the wave,
snow blanches the tips,
the curl
becomes contours.

It could ascend higher than the sky
and blind the sun,
immerse our heads
and blacken our vision.

The blue heart
swells to the horizon,
the far distance explores the center

in the issuance
from the depths,
one massive embodiment animates increase,
constrains the effusion
of perpetuity

lasts long
as a prayer for it to recede.

1830–33, Katsushika Hokusai
Hokusai Museum, Tokyo

LANDSCAPE WITH A CLUMP OF TREES

Carve a niche in the landscape

light divorced from the memory of childbirth,
the smell of damp rags
and blood smudging the floor.

Evince a shadow around the edges

a lacuna admitting fresh air,
the sensitive accompaniment
of an animal and the land,
a butterfly and a flower,
a milk white hand and a dewdrop.

Effect the clouds encircling the center

the barrier to Luciferic interference

the numinous articulated quietly,
the ethereal not interfered with,
the bucolic as only the divine could touch
without clamor

free to express their own radiant center
devoid of clanging machines,
the reflection of brute force,

the gutter debouching in mid-stream,
keen eyes burning at the high point.

Enhance on each leaf
an aura mingling lucence and ripe green

the reflection of grass ripped,
crushed and eaten.

Elucidate a solitary bubble on a tadpole's tail,
the croak
of an old frog

the refusal to plunge before noon.

1844, Théodore Rousseau
National Gallery of Victoria, Melbourne

RAIN, STEAM AND SPEED

Rushing headlong through a haze of past
conjoined with future knowing no advance
other than this dimension,
no meaning to the mass
of speed,
violent discharge,
roar encompassing the beating heart
in confusion,
miasma,
nonsensical passion,
obliteration of finer sensitivity

no inkling that we don't belong

we'll surpass the metallic hiss
and shudder

the apocalyptic absence of coarse grit,
snarl, and coke

scented light washing away grime,
the knell
breaking in the aftermath of avarice

wheels spinning
elsewhere than submission
to worldliness.

1844, William Turner
National Gallery, London

MONGOLIAN INVASION

Withstand the attack.

From out of the dark
they clot the skies
and pollute the tide.

From black land
with irreverent purpose they advance
to destroy and blind children.

From a corrupt heart
the stain reaches a koto's lone note,
the moon's retreat,
lovers on the windward side

until swept away.

1847, Kikushi Yosai
National Museum, Tokyo

BOSTON HARBOR

Ready to acquiesce
to the balm suffusing all matter
with tenderness born in a mother's bosom,
an unearthly fire
suspended on the portal
between the Muse holding aloft
her blazing scepter
and the hues in my soul

on an unquenchable flume radiating heat,
when light strains to part
from the higher orb
and descend
to filter between outstretched arms
invoking the fulsome charge
of the divine
and dusk substituting lame oration
for brilliance,
a marriage with heaven.

1850–55, Fitz Henry Lane
Museum of Fine Arts, Boston, Massachusetts

ROMANS OF THE DECADENCE

In a gown of stained white
I'll slumber until blood congeals in an egg,
fledglings hatch
and drown
in wine.

In a bubble leaking from bruised pores
I'll reach a nostril and burst.
My scent will be of aching flesh,
languor
and afterbirth cloying as frog spawn,
fluid as honey.

Venus will wave goodbye,
Aphrodite shake her head,
a mistress plucked from a harem
and offered to the potentate on a throne
adulate her lot
than mine.

Bells tinkle
on bedclothes,
grapes crush between teeth,
gullets move up and down.

Oh,
for one hour in a plain room,
I want to cuddle my mother again.

1850, Anselm Feuerbach
Augustiner Museum, Freiburg, Germany

OPHELIA

Who would suppose
she would have relinquished the tender twist
in her womb
to drown at the foot of the well,
drifting into the heart.

She sang:
Will you carry me with my bouquet
to fairyland bearing lanterns,
and mist nymphets singing:

Blue thread joining blanched lips,
peach juice in between,
luminous eyes adoring bangles fit
for the devil's queen

saliva and ghost breath congealed on a platter,
forever born in secret arbors
the elusive form of life preserving matter.

Will you pray for me
while I die here?

A question.
Why is it we barely rise before we sink?

The quiet turning around.

The bottom waits for you,
Ophelia.

1851–1852, John Millais
Tate Britain, London

PAYSAGE HUILE SUR TOILE

A frozen,
harmless night divulging the lisp
of clarity over stone,
moist cry,
black swallow
as she moves tenderly amongst the leaves.

1855, Gustave Courbet
Kunsthalle Friart, Fribourg, Switzerland

END OF THE HAMLET OF GRUCHY

Fathoms beneath my feet, the sea roars at night,
batters the rocks,
and leaves debris on the shoreline.

I care not for wine, manna from heaven,
or carved implements to pick up slivers of meat,
only a white sail on the horizon
when you approach, my sweet.

The wind tears at the leaves
of the old tree, tries to uproot it
decade after decade, strip it of vitality.

I am not interested
in sky high fortresses repelling invaders,
mansions
or salt encrusted abodes casting shadows
on ice,
only decent life
when you return, my love.

The silence surrounds us like water
in a dream,
the stone wall catches the sun's glint,
and the clouds fashion into puffs
that would befit a goddess hiding her breast
from the gaze of disinterred wraiths.

I have no need for words
born in the flush of heat,
symphonies
or transcendent works of art,
only the look in your eyes
when you hold your son,
my darling.

1856, Jean-Francois Millet
Museum of Fine Arts, Boston, Massachusetts

MADAME MOITESSIER

A shadow will retreat
and leave an effigy of paradise
in its wake,
a raindrop burst
and trickle patterns likened to the imprint
of a deity
on Spring, an iris open
and gaze
into the eyes delighting in a fleck
of light on a curve

sunset will rupture
and inspire a rose in bloom,
Aphrodite's vial spill
and stain lips
with nectar fulfilling a man's fancy,
a cloud unfold
and protect a body
from the carnal intensity
of wind
from the east

the luminous orb traversing the blue sky,
resplendent
in a manner befitting a solitary queen
will,
even after setting in the formless black night,

blanch an aura around a heart
in full repose
silently beating.

1856, Jean Auguste Dominique Ingres
National Gallery, London

THE NEAPOLITAN FISHER BOY

Concentrate,
and what is revealed?
The screech of a gull in flight,
the sea rolling on a beach,
the scuttle
of crabs to reach holes dotting the tideline

the seamstress's lewd cry
as a suitor approaches her door.

Imagine even more
as a hollow shell divulges its secrets:

a monstrous wave carrying a ship
to doom,
whale spume splashing on her back,
the yawn of a trader
after twenty-four hours
at sea

the blissful sigh when her lover leaves.

1857–1858, Jean-Baptiste Carpeaux
The National Museum of Western Art, Tokyo

ANGELICA AND THE WOUNDED MEDORO

I have salve to tend to your wounds—
the sweat between my breasts,
an abode for you to rest—
my intimate lap,
a secure place to heal
before the world calls you to fight again—
my arms.

Though you may be bleeding,
barely able to lift your head,
the vultures circling beyond the mountain pass,
I am certain providence will bare light
in your heart

it shan't be long
before we are entwined,
your blood staining my thighs,
the trial shall be over
as soon as the moon shines on our entanglement,
your flesh closing and my lips open

the blessed song of consummation
will pass over our bodies huddled beneath an oak,
the last sear of pain transforming into ecstatic groans

you will fall not to hard earth,
but with the delectable swoon

of a martyr into heavenly reward,
into the palpitating languor
of my bosom.

1860, Eugène Delacroix
Art Gallery of New South Wales, Sydney

OEDIPUS AND THE SPHYNX

Beware of the tiger, she lurks
and preys upon your pride
and touches your heart with vanity.

Am I so inebriated with your spell
I would turn from truth
for the sake of bringing about union
with material being?
Am I so ingrained in the darkeners
I would surrender my intellect
for the mere pleasure of touching your body?

To deny me will be your end,
to love me will be your salvation.

Do your really think I would abandon my duty,
return to base need,
plunge deeply into your flesh?

I'll enter your place of rest,
slide gently between your bones,
substitute black droplets
for the seed of new generations.

I'll escape your clinging to my body,
cast off your vice,
seek the highest wishes of the eternal spirit:

You are only a siren
who would control the ground
of desire
and taster the dregs of lust
where they lie unashamed
before the altar of delight.

Do you believe I can sustain the murmuring
of your spirit?

NOT AT ALL!

1860, Gustave Moreau
Metropolitan Museum of Art, New York

PAOLO AND FRANCESCA DA RIMINI

Flood me with the scent born in a rose,
wash me with dew lit up on a thorn,
embrace me
with tendrils entwining a nightingale's throat

wet lips taste
of Spring,
the solstice becalms the tide
before froth begins to flow,
numb fingers fondle an open web.

Drown my eyes
in powder and mist,
purge the ache
from my chilblains,
surrender heart and furrow
to an idol glistening in the storm

malign limpets overshadow the swoon,
darken clouds

maudlin figments cling to the vine,
express discontent at the tryst

inclement witnesses,
virtue their hope,
condemnation their zeal,

in the saturation of bliss aligning stars
forever thankful
for the entourage of sun and moon,
lie down and weep.

1867, Dante Gabriel Rossetti
National Gallery of Victoria, Melbourne

THE WALK

Numinous black night,
let your cadaver grace our silk
with your tones,
our demeanor
with traces of somnolence,
foliage
with prescience:

If you ignore Hades saturating every bough,
your skin will survive the resurrection
from the dead,
your bones still pace the solemn woods,
your feet crunch leaves and flowers

when the light banishes shadow
and the golden city
free of rain and ice absorbs darkness
like a child gobbling a sweet,
you'll put away your parasols
and having no use of powder and shade
allow my eye to bury in your core.

1871, Paul Cézanne
The National Museum of Western Art, Tokyo

NOCTURNE: BLUE AND SILVER- CHELSEA

With one swathe of dusk,
should I obliterate the lives behind the lights,
annihilate idleness, allow the sallow glow
to reflect brains smeared to paste,
or leave them to wallow in torpor

in the haze of nonchalance,
destroy the observer who,
for all he cares, has nothing
to add to the night,
merely the passive fruit
of silence
and the sluggish water drowning memories
of its source bubbling from rocks,
or leave him
to stand
as if the moon could douche his blood
with an echo from centuries
when the wail of a baby was heard

in a fit of pique, dissolve blackness itself,
and leave a pallor reminding us
of skulls
and bones left in the sun to dry

accept his heart beats in unknown darkness,
and should be brought to the surface

to resist the bright energy
that, severe as the furnace below,
would immolate inner mystery
in a blazing eye?

1871, James Abbott Mc Neill Whistler
Tate Gallery, London

LAKE NEMI

Willing to ebb,
to dissipate,
to partake faintly where the sun dies,
the music wanes,
and the falling wind carries me
to the ground below my feet

to mountains of pain building within the temple,
which will fall
if I allow her to.

Valiantly attempting to still the onward shades
of palsy,
frightened tenderness,
blunt nerves defining numbness.

Willing to infuse nascent blood
with heat lingering in sunset,
cast off the burden which arrived early
and obscured the raiment of aftershine

to join the warrior beyond alms strewn
from paradise

if only I'd been able
to withstand the mortal coil.

1872, George Innes
Museum of Fine Arts, Boston, Massachusetts

THE TROUT

A sanguine breath filtering a network
of unwarmed veins,
An inquisitive underlip.
Tentative, watchful eyes.
Nuclei in transparent mucus.
Wondering.
Where is he?
Where?
Drifting silently.
Belonging to the unseen,
untamed below.
Icy
a whisper coiling the emerald waters:

"A solitary person will eat your tenderness."

1872, Gustave Courbet
Kunsthaus, Zurich, Switzerland

SALOME AT THE PRISON

Glisten
on the puddle, stain the walls
with a dead aura

light,
barely arising from comprehension
in darkness,
revealing a dungeon disease eats

inebriate shadow under her eyes
with a glimmer, cloy the dank heartache odor
in the rose

the tomb filling with reek older
than Abel's wound

stuff sweat in each nostril,
catch breath escaping a chink between bricks

Satanic blood welling into nerve endings,
flooding her brain

drowning the voice of conscience.

1873–76, Gustave Moreau
The National Museum of Western Art, Tokyo

SNOW AT LOUVECIENNES

Cessation of breath
or a backdrop
for a snowdrop?
Deaf white repression
or blind substance offering Spring?
Blanket on a tomb
or Aphrodite's hard glance before arousal?

Gelid fields will receive another layer,
windows shut tightly against the cold

a solitary visitant
whose blood will still pour through fiery veins,
take it upon herself,
even if her feet freeze
or her nose drops off,
to deliver patented tinctures
to an ailing friend shivering under a quilt.

1874, Alfred Sisley
(The Phillips Collection, Washington)
Hayward Gallery, London

GOING TO EVENING CHURCH

Timbres of remorse,
vocalese pronouncing regret, paeans
uttered in Heaven's descent mingle
and shroud an evening trail to the altar

wisps
of orange and blue,
tints of leaf green,
the breeze rustling corn ears meld
and follow the procession
to worship

latent cries
of the dead, heartbeats of the living,
whispers
in an open bosom gather in one hue
and guide the next step
on the path to an open door

numinous wings entangled in a web,
gilded messengers bound to the earth
for a second,
earnest eyes
determined to drink the lessons
of Scripture
sense eternal revival
and join in the one body

known

to be not alone.

1874, Samuel Palmer
Art Gallery of New South Wales, Sydney

PORTRAIT OF RENEE DELMAS DE PONT-JEST

Allow me to express a solemn promise.
When the ink runs dry,
I shall scrape hard into the page
and leave the remnant
of inspiration.

Beauty torn from a smoldering heart
is an evanescent,
mercurial appearance
no one can instantiate.

Finery abstracted from the finger that wove,
twisted and pulled it
into a shape that clings to lissome curves
is only ephemeral tissue hanging in a cloudless sky.

Even if they convey the glow
of lilac refreshing a gown,
the similitude
of flowers entwining hair,
or the intensity
of light destroying the black underneath,
words scrawled quick as rain,
but divorced from the wellspring

eternity is known to raise,
need not be written.

1875, Louise Abbema
National Gallery of Victoria, Melbourne

WOMAN IN BLACK

How should I make my entrance?
Enough for enamored guests
to apprise my apparel,
but not to linger and lead hovering lips
into the mist of vanity.

How must I address the most important personage
in the room?
With warmth and seriousness,
enough to single me out as a well-bred,
highly civilized young woman,
but not effusive,
bringing accusations of forwardness
unfit for a daughter of illustrious means.

How shall I display to its full effect
the ravishing quality of an evening dress?
In the ambit of bright light,
but faintly near the shadow,
enough to render the roses pink
as the blooms we pick in May,
the folds deep and exquisite
as a valley
in Spring

enhanced
with the dark secrets of the divine,

but not fully exposed in the glare,
declare that no one else,
not even a queen
of beauty
or Aphrodite's glistening skin could outweigh my presence
on a gladsome night inviting the stars
to earth.

1875, Berthe Morisot
National Museum of Western Art, Tokyo

CÔTE DES BOEUFS AT L'HERMITAGE

Bleed into their lives
and they may return a moist glance
of hope,
channel vigor into their abode
and they may brighten the walls
and polish the windows,
invest energy into the undergrowth
and they may defy the will
of a landowner to raise it by the roots.

Imbue each leaf with a force of identity
and they may turn to face an ambiance
conjoining radiance and subliminal light,
leave alone the watery sky
and it may reveal it has no need
to conjoin smoke, cinders and a pall
from distant works

but in freedom to increase
and decrease as the breath
of nature has always sustained it,
may provide nourishment to the trees
sheltering a lowly house

from the acquisitive predilections
of ghouls parading as men.

1877, Camille Pissarro
National Gallery, London

JEWS PRAYING IN THE SYNAGOGUE AT YOM KIPPUR

Forlorn,
I feel the separation.
I am helpless
and abuse light in the coil
of suffering.
The marrow in my spine knows no rest,
the fluid in my brain no meaning.
If only I hadn't ignored the dignitary passing by
on the cobbles.
I pretend I am worthy—my skin should be flailed,
my tongue hung out in the rain.
Leave me to wander on soiled pasture,
leave me to bloat like the carcass,
leave me to feed the crows.
I enter the cloud,
smell the sulphur,
look into dead black eyes.

In one voice.

Can I atone?

Bring me into the fold. Flush out my veins.
Silence the throb
in my neck.

1878, Maurycy Gottlieb
Tel Aviv Museum of Art, Israel

ISLAND OF THE DEAD

Whispers transfused into insensibility,
mollusk clinging to wet skin,
chill flesh dulled in pallor,

Silence.

The slip of an oar blanketed in stealth,
the growth of a tree surrounded by stone,
the entrance
to night shadowed by darkness.

Silence.

An oft visited crag swooning in moonlight,
a transient coffin shrouded in secrecy,
the numinous past,
gelid
and tempted by Hades into complete submission.

Silence.

1880, Arnold Böcklin
The Metropolitan Museum of Art, New York

THE TEA

Delightful.
Each sip evokes the dusk
of China

a temple in fading light,
lanterns brightening a pathway
through incense,
the steep steps leading to a forbidden statue.

Your tea set fit
for a queen's dainty hands.

The retinue in red, a crown of pearls,
the magical luster
as the bells
in the cathedral ring the interior into your breast.

We're two ordinary girls
on an ordinary day
who, in our ordinary way,
can elicit the secrets of an empire,
the struggles of a dominion
and, in the ambience lingering over the tea in a cup,
substitute dowd
and lethargy

with the high-spirited dance in white frocks
and golden slippers.

1880, Mary Cassatt
Museum of Fine Arts, Boston, Massachusetts

THREE DANCERS IN THE WINGS

Supple as a swan's neck I could bend my arms,
pirouette on tiptoes until the petals beneath
fear the depth of a bruise

with one leap, untrammeled by the earth's pull
to the center, reach Saturn's rings
and transfer their chill to my cheekbones

but he only wants to taste the scent
behind my ear.

From the confinement of taut flesh
ready to receive the mantle
of free flight,
I could break the bonds with incarceration
and tempt the sun to let me enter her aura

burned through to the quick,
in a downdraft reminiscent of a fluttering bird,
descend once more into slippered feet

but he only wants to imprint his thumb
on an ankle out of sight.

I could glide from blood welling in my heart
to a white dove released in aether,
fraternize with disembodied sylphs

before apotheosis, distress carnal need
with the abnegation of density
close to the eye blackened in rotting fruit

but he, a seed in the pulp, can only say:

"I'll meet you at ten."

1880–85, Edgar Degas
The National Museum of Western Art, Tokyo

THE CLIFF AT FÉCAMP

Boats speed
hither, blades
of glass.
Sprites,
shifting,
echo.

Spring!

Spirit
out
of reach of sunset.

Lift!

Wind blow.

Take me...

1881, Claude Monet
Aberdeen Art Gallery, Scotland

LUNCHEON OF THE BOATING PARTY

Candor,
elegance, rapprochement.
Whoever you are,
whatever your status,
you'll blend in a harmony
of texture, color,
and a place reserved for you alone.

Simplicity, bonhomie,
gaiety.
In spite of the rain forecast later
to pelt down with force,
you'll titillate each other
with trivia,
describe the light bouncing from the ripples,
and eschew the dark smudge barely in focus.

Insouciance,
carelessness, sanguinity.
Not every day can be spent this way.
For an hour or so,
divested of the crude need
to oil the machine demanding toil,
you can close the door
on a stuffy interior,

throw away the key
and invite a stranger out into the open.

1881, Pierre-Auguste Renoir
(The Phillips Collection, Washington)
Hayward Gallery, London

THE THINKER

Am I the embodiment of a god
or a long-suffering mortal
far removed from divine insight?

Foliage is fresh and green, fragrance pure,
insects hum and make trails.

Do I penetrate the essence of being
or merely rest on the surface
as a cloud on a mountain?

Birds twitter under clogged eaves,
volumes of water pour through the sluice,
a clock announces the time- midday.

Have I discovered the reason
why I meditate so deeply
or does nothing appear
in the recesses behind my brow?

The cause of a flutter is a leaf,
the abrasion under my thigh
a hard rock,
the glare on my pate a yellow sun.

Do I have significance,
a definite purpose

in the mélange of grief
and blood
or am I dispensable, easily forgotten,
a lonely instant before expiration?

A comet's tail lengthened the other night,
a star shone brighter than I'd seen it before,
the moon shimmered in an aura
I took to be equally mysterious
as the glow in my heart.

1881–82 (model), Auguste Rodin
The National Museum of Western Art, Tokyo

A BAR AT THE FOLIES-BERGÈRE

Listless as a lizard in the broiling sun,
bereft of the spark enabling a fire
to illuminate cat's eyes,
I'll position her at a distance from my dying glands

lackluster
in the malady draining spirit from an inner well,
devoid of verdancy flowering in mist,
I'll turn her from my bleak stare

dolorous in the drip of blood
from my skin
to the rose, inert
on the nubile curves that thresh
and arch in ecstasy,
I'll mismatch her potency
with the weakness of my brain.

Clarity contrasts with fantasy
of a clearer beyond,
gaiety bruises the tenderness of my nerves,
the blare
of a musician rising to a climax
slices a pathway between my ears.

Years ago,
I could have offered her a tip piercing idyll,

pink coverlets
and a sip of champagne

now,
only a damp cloth to wipe my brow,
a cup
to catch my phlegm

in the aftermath
of cough
and splutter,
a mirror to view her lips free of spittle.

1882, Edouard Manet
Courtauld Gallery, London

BATHERS AT ASNIÈRES

Consider,
if the world stopped in orbit,
the moon froze,
the sun at the apex refused to shift one inch,
and everybody held the fascination
of the Medusa's stare,
where white bergs dissociate from their brethren,
would we prefer a life drained of blood

in a minimalistic trance,
free
of the pulse leading to the clash
of steel, subsist
in quietude
and feel no pain

in the absence of ecstasies,
scintillating beams emanating from our hearts,
wait in the one proud moment
of immobility,
cessation of heat,
ardor and lividity,
until,
inevitably,

as would be our fate
the crushing wheel would roll on?

1884, Georges Seurat
National Gallery, London

COOLING OFF AT SHIJO

If only
I could slip even further
beyond my calves,
watch the bubbles pop
and my eyes breathe dulcet blue

lost in cool waves,
wash away the rouge
and shadow,
let my garments float
until drenched
and sink

under the gleam of moonlight
frozen in the heat,
rise purified
and clean of the scent
of every man
who has touched my flesh.

1885, Yoshitoshi Tsukioka
Ota Memorial Museum of Art, Tokyo

MOON AT THE PLEASURE QUARTERS

Let us drift with the petals,
show pleasure under lamplight,
blanche with the moon's purity

show we belong
in pink fluttering to the floor,
rouge staining our cheeks,
the fruitful association with strangers

the climate conducive to growth,
the ambience perpetual in short lived liaison,
the shadow nonchalant as a rainbow,
deep as a bow across a string

we will survive the next winter,
feel the ice on our feet,
the mist in our hair

on the turning to spring,
await with knitted brow
and irregular sighs
the bloom invoking delight
in many men's eyes.

1886, Yoshitoshi Tsukioka
Ota Memorial Museum of Art, Tokyo

VIEW FROM MONTMARTRE

Anxious not to countenance facile embellishment,
I reveal the bloodless Paris,
the darker brooding Paris
which lingers below me,

tread the wary depths
and force feed each child
with the hope they will rise above the cruelty,
each bloated street walker mingle in the firmament
barley visible through the clouds

still holding a ragged brush,
terminate the abode
in the light that barely seeps into caverns,
ditches, and abandoned sheds
where rats nibble at rags and pillow stuffing

smear the exterior with the inevitable entrapment
that could reflect back,
if only hidden under the gloom,
the structures that make up
the possible exit
into a similar world
devoid of entry into this one.

1886, Vincent Van Gogh
Kunstmuseum, Basle, Switzerland

THE MONTAGNE SAINTE-VICTOIRE WITH A LARGE PINE

Smear a brain on absence till it arises as a peak,
scrape an iris in the wind
until it bends into a tree,
unravel skin into patches forming a living vista

the view will beat with the same rhythm
a voyeur extracts in the uplift
and descent of an arm.

Build an abode
as you would a temple in your spine,
construct a bridge with the bones in your feet,
a hollow
with the void between your eyes,
a hillock with a lump
on your chest

the glimmer in memory
will rise to meet dawn illuminating a bole,
the translucent leap from a lachrymose childhood
to an adult tear
saturate a cloud

the inscrutable interior dark as Hades,
raise an outline

into the purview
of a witness.

1887, Paul Cézanne
The Courtauld Gallery, London

SELF PORTRAIT BEFORE EASEL

I seek to expose the inchoate source
found to underlie the surface
where, unrepentant and fully unconcerned
with waves of bloodlight, a swirling sun,
the mad attempt at dominating me,
I'll gaze at you,
a form shimmering in the distance

the absence of black on white
or white on black,
the glare of a suffering child
who, misappropriated with the joy
fresh canals and free flowing ducts can give,
stumbles through acres of stubble,
burnt chaff
and the echo of a tortured ancestor
calling him to desist from divulging the pain
with open eyes

1888, Vincent Van Gogh
Van Gogh Museum, Amsterdam

RAVINE

Cushioned from the delinquent force
by prefiguring a gust between my eyes,
and channeling it through my fingers

corrosion,
leering unblinkered at the core

inevitable annihilation,
focusing intently on a bird's swirl to earth,
the thrust into blue,
the drop into the rage
between the clefts

the Creator constrained in a square inch,
the shadow in a jot,
the entirety in a sliver,
the cosmos in a drop of blood
squeezed from a rock.

There is nothing, absolutely nothing
to keep me from calling out:

"Manacled calves
back lashed."

1889, Vincent Van Gogh
Museum of Fine Arts, Boston, Massachusetts

FIELD OF POPPIES NEAR GIVERNY

The chance
when I danced
and forbade carefulness:

Ariadne's golden tress leaking into stems,
the deft hand of Eros passing over unburied fields,
the swift eye of Orpheus marking the space
where Titans stained the fields with almost forgotten battles

the freshness of blue leaping into my heart
and erasing the pallor,
green stifling a race toward unbelievability
and caressing the tips,
light imprinting on my spine
the cause I should engender:

the effect bright
as day losing all connection
with the night.

1890, Claude Monet
Museum of Fine Arts, Boston, Massachusetts

NEAR HEIDELBERG

Conscious of the way,
the pleasure.
Listen, ineffable silence.
Listen, the trees.
Flowing life.
Listen, the wind.
Rushing spirit.
Listen to the roar in the leaves,
the flight of the clouds

from behind the tangible canvas
the power revealing the dream.

Accept no being without hearing the return.
Take!
Seize!
Erect it, and stand to face
the inevitable conclusion of my desire,
the intangible edge.

Conscious of the vague hint of bliss,
conscious of my heart telling me
the way forward–

the intimations of light I can reveal–

into the spirit charged, constant striving
to see you surveying the dream

and meld my heart in yours.

1890, Arthur Streeton
National Gallery of Victoria, Melbourne

THE ROAD TO COPENHAGEN FROM KASTRUP

The bloodless odor of cold,
a hint of woodsmoke,
the near to death taste
of a shadow.

How long must I prolong endurance?

The earthy clucks of a hen,
the barely audible shift of a cloud,
the squeak
as a widow tightens her door.

Through a shiver,
I'll plant my frozen feet and persevere.

Blue like mountain ice
descends upon the world,
light reticent as the sun to illumine Pluto
divulges the squares
of human retreat

gaunt with the travail of hard roots
and gelid sap,
an old tree shows no sign of rejuvenation.

Forever, though,
if I had my way,
I would stand in this stark beauty

allow the exterior to numb my faculties,
so determined
to escape into a wall
of flame.

1890, Theodor Philipsen
State Museum for Art, Copenhagen, Denmark

THE STREETWALKER

I dance with satyrs,
barely escape the supping
of an incubus,
lie inert
while a monster seeks the red spot
in my heart

the empty streets
are no place for a child.

White water sprinkles on my thighs,
the dove flutters above my brow,
harpsichords construct melodies swirling the silk
of Chinese boudoirs

I know I have lived as a queen.

A rosebud blights in the south wind,
a smelly cloud stains feathers,
beetles crack open
and spill yellow insides

can you look at me
for more than a minute?

1890–91, Henri Toulouse Lautrec
The Metropolitan Museum of Art, New York

YOUNG GIRL WITH A HEN

Don't step on the sun,
it will burn your toes.
Don't taste the moon,
the blemishes will make you ill.
Avoid drinking cloud milk,
the white will curdle in your throat.

The chicken likes rhubarb leaves
shredded
with thyme.

Wear clothes snug as bark wrapping a trunk,
keep your shoes on
through the grit
and mud.
Pluck a flower to savor its fragrance.

Feathers are scant protection in a blizzard.

Think of orbs swirling in outer dimensions.
Imagine paradise
warm as a fire on a cold night.
Realize the future
abundant with a Muse heralding new words
that create blue eyes,
red dresses,
and rainbows as soon as you speak them.

Beady eyes, black as the dark hiding ghouls,
imps,
and monsters mummy protects you from,
only spy dusty wheat
thrown from your hand.

1890, Maurice Denis
The National Museum of Western Art, Tokyo

CROUCHING WOMAN

The weight of morbidity
foisted on living tissue
and the simultaneous need
to escape.

Restriction on her carriage
by the fact of limitation,
constraint,
and necessity enforced from creation
according to divine image,
and freedom
to bend into any shape
she desires'

a shadow reflection
of the infinite
unable to reach unbounded horizons
alone,
and the mercurial spirit
which can surpass the weakness
of bodily deformation
with one leap
of untrammeled consciousness.

1891, Auguste Rodin
Victoria and Albert Museum, London

SHEEP IN A SNOWSTORM

A tempest
from the nether region
like breath from Hell splitting perception?
No one can withstand the savagery,
no one has the strength.

An immensity of power lacerating my skin,
pockmarking my cheeks?
No one knows who is at the helm, no one can assuage its relentlessness
to annihilate the focal point to survive before its onslaught.

A punishment
for thinking I am strong
and able to control the direction
from which it issues?
The injured forbearer
hurling my body into the drift behind
waiting to claim it
for another lifetime?

1892–93, Joseph Farquharson
Aberdeen Art Gallery, Scotland

IN A CORNER ON THE MACINTYRE

So what
if the crevices hold darkness
barely touched by the light,
the river winds
on an unremarkable path
broken by a steep incline,
the trees stand almost without support
above their reflection?

Rabid eyes care naught
for the illusion
of sacred earth shedding an intolerable will
and settling into quietude
unbounded in depth,
mesmerizing in potency,
dulcet in tonality.

It's out of the question
to answer how finality belongs to change:

bedrock formed by centuries of wear,
moisture lifted in warm air,
color softened
and made brilliant
by the alternation of hard sun
and transient moon

smoke from a gun disappearing into the blue.

1895, Tom Roberts
National Gallery of Australia, Canberra

NEVERMORE

The moon in her bones,
the placid sea in her breast,
a raven in her brain.

They harp and squawk incessantly:

"What right
has she to display every curve
and recess?"

A yellow pillow like a mirage
beneath her face,
flowers embroidered from the netherworld
beneath her form,
woodwork carved from an ancient impulse
following her lines.

Luminous scent gliding in the window,
edible colors staining the wall,
transcendent realms burying slumber in a pose.

The black in my eyes black as the bird,
the ache in my loins blue as the sky,
the vitriol on their lips
red as the sunset on a burning tree.

Nevermore
a riding boot on a foot,
the plague in a womb,
drift from smoke
and haze

a tangle of wires abuzz with news.

1897, Paul Gaugin
Courtauld Gallery, London

THE BOULEVARD MONTMARTRE AT NIGHT

People sluiced from Neptune
and left dripping on a path,
light transported from the moon
and smoldering on a slick, black night,
the entrance to Hades
opened in a window
and inviting fragrance of wet smoke.

Profligate, can you survive?

The babble of drunk lips
and insults hurled into the air,
the slither of night carts
and the pop of bottles uncorked,
ladies huddled in an alcove
and gentlemen fondling fronds.

Watcher, are you still aware?

The blare reaching Arcadia's portal
and bruising the ears of a sylph,
the translation of primrose
to grime smearing every face
and discharging smudge
into blood

the deadly cough chewing the lungs
and swallowing rain.

Paris, are you still alive?

1897, Camille Pissarro
National Gallery, London

CHRYSANTHEMUMS

Blossoms.
Perfume piquant.

Seek the utterance embraced by wind,
the first whisper contained in an echo:

"Hera and Zeus in collusion with the moon."

Strive to render each luminous hue
in accordance with natural becoming,
the embodiment of ecstasy and joy:

cerulean mistress, ardor tempting Heaven.

Surrender to freedom,
the precious substance they instantiate:

Lucifer's light beyond our light.

Bud to the love
they engender,
the fertile repose before sunset.

The transcendent burst in midnight
and plenum, lucent within.

1897, Claude Monet
Fine Arts Museum, Basel, Switzerland

PAN READING TO A WOMAN BY A BROOK

In delirious days by the river,
a magic aura precluding reason,
I watch their tryst,
and, like a voyeur
banished from Israel incarnate,
read his lips.

"The vein in my soul bleeds into a jewel.

Shall I pour into your body
and splay the plums with moonlight,
effect the carnal
with mellifluous dips,
bloat your vision with dreams
of bliss.

Shall we dine on victuals stolen from the sea—
oysters plump and tender, mussel fibers torn free.
Moist glands you'll surrender in the feast of love,
tantalizing sweetbread twisted from the dove.

An eye socket blue with fever,
fingertips white with rain,

toes crinkled in a bath,
sandalwood gorging a brain."

1898, Aubrey Beardsley
Brighton and Hove Museum, England

've # 20th Century

NOTRE DAME

Is it only a wound that bleeds into my brush,
a messy under womb leaving drops on my palette,
an eviscerated incarnate smearing entrails
and lips over apses and glass

merely,
the flailed remains of one taken early,
an unfocussed rise
of a saint delivering eulogies to dead martyrs
into an equally undistinguishable sky?

We care not
for the sharp clanging at doomsday,
an impeccable chalice glinting in candlelight,
the maudlin dirge emanating from height surpassing frowst

but,
within,
an oblique ray shattering on marble,
gilt edged columns penetrating the moon,
the murk
of yesterday's squalor meeting the melting temple in the heart,

a pink and rose petal
in the mish mash
of embodiment.

1900, Henri Matisse
Tate Gallery, London

SUMMIT OF THE KING WILLIAM RANGE

Bleakness, hard light and cloud.

the canvas cannot hold the exquisite remains
of upheaval,
let alone portray the blind stasis
of impenetrable rock.

Cold,
bright reflection
and angular formation

the breath of solitude is unable to imbue the silence
with warmth,
nor infuse the vista
with belonging.

Cracks,
boulders
and the unerring sense time has stilled,
and belongs in pre-Cambrian inertia,
than to the fluttering
and chattering below the snow line

cruelty doesn't belong here,
nor tired lips and expiration.

The bland summit devoid of life
accepting bright water into culverts,
adopting raw wind scouring the terrain

under the moist film,
an eye, refuses to divulge
how it came
to be.

1902, William Piguenit
Tasmanian Museum and Art Gallery, Hobart

CHATEAU NOIR

From an ancient woodland, blow the scent
of bracken
and toadstool through an open window

from a door ajar, allow the perfume
of a mistress's boudoir
to mingle in the shadows under an elm

permeate the stone
with the grit under my fingernails,
enable the mortar
tightened between bricks
to encrust the softness in my hands

as night imprints bark
and leaves,
make sure it pronounces a Kingdom
of the sacred underworld
in every room and corridor

with the concoction
of spice
and candlelight bubbling on a stove,
ensure the aroma congeals in a paste
I can smear on the sky

intoxicated
with the breath
of mountain air suffusing every glade,
enable it
to fill the lungs of a resident in her bath

in return,
as she powders her cheeks
and files her nails,
suck the dust into a palette

evince the solidity of her home.

1903–4, Paul Cézanne
Museum of Modern Art, New York

PEGASUS

There are no fields left on which to gallop,
at least
wide enough
for unbridled spurts
and carefree romps

the soil clogged, the grass lank
and damp, the lea spread with fungus

the clouds a soft footfall,
the mist
a gateway,
the mountain a course to stretch your legs

beyond the sun,
an even higher ground
to leave a vague imprint,
an uncluttered acreage to breach extremities,
a clearer expanse to spread your wings

the limit in excess
of the unlimited bounds outside the boundary,
strictures imperceivable

you can hear the echo
of predecessors surpassing birth,
triumph

of offspring eschewing a clammy finger
upon a mane,
transcend flesh incarcerating a pulse

blood growing cold
in winter,
reins
held by a wide eyed human.

1900–5, Odilon Redon
National Gallery of Victoria, Melbourne

THE BLIND MAN'S MEAL

Taste the pale ghost as she settles on a palette,
the stringent drops squeezed from the Master's veins,
the blue air an angel weeps
as she descends
in the pulse that could drown her sight.

With this hand,
solitary
as the other, which seek its other
just as tenderly,
touch the dead crumb a mourner would leave
when he brushes off the farewell meal under the gallows,
the earthenware a bibulous swine would fill
on a journey
from the stye
to an outlying planet devoid of heat.

Reminiscent
of the abrupt rise of a penitent after the holy feast,
the glide of a tongue over a lip
as remnants
are cleaned from the plane of matter,
hear the scrape of a foot

in the tomb lit night,
harboring the wishes of sainthood
for an embodied eye,

a demon for an empty socket,
one of our kind,
between hoary bed
and leaking roof,
giving thanks.

1903, Pablo Picasso
The Metropolitan Museum of Art, New York

SAILING BOATS AT CHATOU

How white is the sail of a boat tacking on the river?

White
as a cloud devoid of rain,
a tabula rasa on which destiny can be flicked,
the supernal view revolving to a higher point over a glacier below.

How red
can a rooftop be when isolated in immobility?
Red as a tongue swallowing pepper,
a cut on a pauper's slaving back,
the heart
of a termagant exposed in daylight.

How blue
the sky, the water
and an eye pinpricked
with green, purple and orange?

Blue
as lapis lazuli crafted by an ancient god,
the Madonna' mourning robes

outside any semblance of high noon,
the deep sea
or gentian petals stained by an inner need
to live,

the delirious figment potentates smear
when they have won the world
for their own use in a paint box.

1906, Maurice de Vlaminck
Art Gallery of New South Wales, Sydney

THE POOL OF LONDON

Paint the Alps
on a raindrop,
an entire civilization in a buttercup

when the clangour
and buzz outreaches the clouds,
burst a rainbow
on smoke and grit.

Daub extraterrestrial blossoms
on a wayfarer's back,
oranges on a swarthy head

as bridges open
and close,
smear the sea with a pathway to oblivion.

Grace a black pipe
with an opposite intended to convey a clean universe,
midnight with a whitewashed plank

oblivious
to dark undercurrents,
reveal a would we'd inhabit at our leisure,
dance on the surface

cauterize burns with light.

1906, André Derain
Tate Gallery, London

L'EAU OU LA BAIGNEUSE

If I touch your foot, it would rock
until every vibration met its opposite in steadiness,
swamp your toes with freshwater,
allow the unending wave upon wave,
thoughtless as a god leaving us alone
and untended,
to reach cloud light reflecting on the surface

ground the embodiment,
let the shimmer subside
and,
static
and inert as Adam's first taste of the apple,
hold the droplets in my throat
for an eon, stroke your shin,
ripple
until every echo in the plane under your skin–

destinies that precede fracture-

rise unabated

immerse you gently,
shift

from silent expanse
into vision without distance.

1907, Frantisek Kupka
Musée National d'Art Moderne, Paris

HOPE, II

The skull
is not the inevitability,
but the mere probability of an erratic birth

the mourners sing not
of the fusion of inert scintilla and rotting flesh,
but merely that the child will form
with cleft palate and contorted bones

the pallor
on her cheeks tells not
of wasted tissue
and limbs abandoned to the gutter

but, on a bright,
clean day,
when her clammy pores secrete white sweat,
and her breasts well
with milk surpassing an underground tomb,
her baby will rise
with fresh blood glistening in sunlight.

1907–8, Gustav Klimt
Museum of Modern Art, New York

LES DEMOISELLES D'AVIGNON

I'll stretch your labia across my cheek,
contort your groin to face the sun,
collapse an orifice
into wet flesh

the pineal gland
an entrance
to a multitude of crimes:

the destitution
of finesse, the abeyance
of culture,
the dissolution of sentience.

I'll place your breast
over the mask of death suppurating dark thoughts,
blind the eye in a black pool
so it seems nothing but a pinprick will shed light

loosen the connection between bud and calyx,
so the flower can renew in aether-

venerable space surpassing wit,
ardor
and chastity

with a gloating hee haw,
abandon the way
you see things

rearrange them to suit my taste.

1907, Pablo Picasso
Museum of Modern Art, New York

THE DOGE'S PALACE SEEN FROM SAN GIORGIO MAGGIORE

Feverish haste on the ripples,
scintillating light on the stone

eternal and chance laden hope mingling beneath.

Flustered and blustery through the shadow,
reflective sun on glass

behind, tinkling cups and drink of blood.

A shift from gold to blue,
the swift recess of crème to white

a halo lingering on a bald head.

Touches of lightness on a cool sky,
intimation of a surface
on primordial depths

a heart determined to forgive a voyeur.

A brush soft as petal,
vision long as a spark on a pulse,
Saturn's countenance avoiding time's suspension
in flight

candelabra illuminating a saint.

1907, Claude Monet
Kunsthaus, Zurich, Switzerland

HOUSES AT L'ESTAQUE

Empty the houses
of owners
and construct until they reach your eyes,
drain the trees
of sap
and bend
until they brush your forehead,
void the sky
and leave it outside space impinging on your brain.

The ground will settle through your loins,
roofs form a tent over your heart,
sidewalls rise until they fill the length
of your back.

If I were brick
I'd build my own steps
to paradise

hard wood,
fashion scaffolding to view my home
from freer plane

a solid cube

as I turn
to face the dull earth

from which I was born to extricate,
balance
on knife edge without falling.

1908, Georges Braque
Kunstmuseum, Berne, Switzerland

STREETLIGHT

Prize the clamps
from my eyes
and I'll penetrate a glutinous web to incandescence,
arrest the dark sheen obscuring my lobes
and I'll assail the doldrums with luminance cleaved from a star,
mask the blood pumping from nether regions
and I'll blaze an aura so intense
the moon will pale
into insignificance,
a firefly disappear
in black dew

a comet, lashing its tail
in the slipstream
of brilliance, hold no clarity
in the brightness
I know persists
in an interior populated by filaments
I'll order
before they become known
as sunrise.

1909, Giacomo Balla
Museum of Modern Art, New York

WORKERS IN THE SNOW

Blood could freeze
on plate glass,
brains stick to a spade

we'll hack our way through black rock
until we reach the sun.

Ice forms clumps in our nostrils,
blue works into our veins

we'll dig
until we reach the furnace demons stoke.

Cold slices between cartilage
and kneecap,
white crunches under our skin

we'll purloin ghostly slaver
from a free man dying of thirst
and warm our sweat.

Saturnine isolation stills the flow
of moisture
to our feet,
toenails curl from hapless flesh,
metal rings

with hymn
of Oreithyia buried a billion miles from a star

as night covers over
what little day remains,
between the drift coaxing our spines
into numbness
and the face hollowing our eyes,
we'll create a furrow leading to daybreak

1910, Edvard Munch
The National Museum of Western Art, Tokyo

GLASS OF ABSINTHE

No bird could fly through the window
and peck
at seeds,
no mouth sip stringent droplets
or cut lips on broken glass

an eye unable to peer
between a laden tray and the ceiling above,
a hand lift a stem
and crack it on a table.

It is no use desiring liquid
that could quench your thirst
or a grape crunch between your teeth

no use,
on a plane
flat as the plain crushed between brown earth
and gravity
so dense it forces an afternoon repast
into dead calm
on a dead surface,
poking your finger

as hard as you can
to find an exit.

1911, Georges Braque
Art Gallery of New South Wales, Sydney

I AND THE VILLAGE

I know how fragile the connection,
how easily broken
the thread between my red pulse
and the bloom on your cheek

how, in an instant, the eternal could lift from a tryst
and leave a mendicant slumbering on pallid grass.

The cycle turns in a slow becoming:

the choke of autumn's smoke in my throat,
the frost on a window

keen wind hardening your skin,
cold watering my eyes

spring blossoms lightening each voice
in the square, fragrance filling desire

summer again:
greeting in the way he has done for half a century:
"Sunflowers turn toward the sun"
a friend, with concern, "Are you well'?

Shall lovers pick daisies by the ford,
glance at the sky and exclaim how blue,
high and clear it is

take each other's hand,
see the topsy turvy, no holds barred look
in the other's eyes

and kiss?

1911, Marc Chagall
Museum of Modern Art, New York

INDIAN TOTEM POLE

Forever after, blood will rise with red flowers,
a green heart sprout on a sward,
dreams prefiguring the last breath
before expiration ascend beyond a rainbow.

Empty my soul into a tree,
assume the agony of childbirth,
the antics of an infant,
the audacity of a youth's venture
into virgin forest.

On the brink of surrender, my breath will pause
with a deep cut into wood, my pulse increase,
my signature trace an ever recurring dance
of leaves under a large sky,
feathers in flight

drunken like a stag in spring
the leap
into the scent of a mate.

Merge my bones
with the talisman
of ancient deities,
cool my feet
in streams straight from pure white snow

in the languorous afternoon heat,
devoid of trappings persisting through iron and glass,
affix my heart
to an embodiment lasting beyond the impulse
to manifest the eternal ground
in whispers,
ephemera,
and puffs under a cloud.

1912, Emily Carr
Art Gallery of New South Wales, Sydney

STREET, BERLIN

With the pink of my tongue
I'll lick open her lips,
the black under my feet
drench every garb hurling toward rare meat
and scallops,
the white
of my eyeball
stain every feather plucked from birds
fortuitous to escape the cold hammer.

Purple
I'll secrete from swollen glands
in fever,
mascara from gel excised from falling locks,
shoes
from the migraine sharp as tin cutting paste.

Pallor belongs to a corpse usurped for the glow
in the theatre's first row

ash, a fire immolating a brain—
powder on a wet cheek

an odour
of stale fish
and mushrooms—
a cadaver

from a bottle tinted green, barely perceived,
the essence
of lily and rose alive in the field
extracted to smudge the aroma
on a hectic night out.

1913, Ernst Ludwig Kirchner
Museum of Modern Art, New York

BOWL OF FRUIT, VIOLIN AND BOTTLE

Eschewing the scent of a final moment,
abnegation
of mortality presupposing a black passage
into darkness,
the Master of Space conjoins sparrow blood
on a stick, a thistle in a womb,
a buttonhole filled with cream.

On a whim,
the Master of Time squeezes Saturn's freezing sweat,
a faun's dance on laudanum,
an Egyptian tomb pregnant with rebirth,
into one instant
far in advance of the voyeur
who supposes he can lick the grime
on individuality.

In contradistinction
to an angel
who descends to enliven each
with the perfection
the divine entrusts to a third dimension,
a Master squashes an instrument,
a receptacle, a source

of nourishment
onto an inert plane that subverts usefulness.

1914, Pablo Picasso
National Gallery, London

WORKSHOP

Conjoin each space
as it appears independently
in a model only the body
divorced from self-satisfaction
could conceive.

Forgo natural perception
for imagination
enacted by a freely spontaneous creative will.

Amplify color
and shadow until anguish underlying machination
manifests in an embodiment disconnected with chaos,
the life in dark regions without a home.

Combine each element
in an harmonious structure
that concentrates order on a plane
that could,
should the void assimilate the inert center,
disappear in oblivion.

1914–15, Wyndham Lewis
Tate Gallery, London

WOMAN COMBING HER HAIR

I'll lengthen the curving which represents a model human
preparing her radiant figure
for observation and scrutiny,
elongate her physique
to accentuate the rhythm which,
voluptuous as Aphrodite and Eros entwined,
is captured
in a moment of pleasure
in preparing to be seen.

With sanguinity born from anticipation
of the mutual rites
she could negate
by a flick of sudden nonchalance,
I'll render concrete the fact
of vitality
she readies herself to prime

open the window, where she'll float
impervious
to the demands of fidelity,
flow with the ripples passing over rills

in her scented room,
cloud the mirror with her breath.

1915, Alexander Archipenko
Tate Gallery, London

WATER LILLIES

Beneath the shimmering surface
there must be something more substantial,
something immanent
in the appearance
upon which I can focus,
something that transcends my inadequate grasp
on the shifting, misty,
forwards and backwards,
hardly capturable elusiveness of it all—

an essence,
a real definition that embodies thusness,
a constant, eternal, undying idea which,
with the love and fluidity in my brush,
I could for an instant capture

if only for a moment,
bring it into for perspective

for a glistening second,
see it in the search outside my soul.

1916, Claude Monet
National Gallery, London

ANNA ZBOROWSKA

If the eyes
are black, molecules disappear,
atoms drench
in absence

indivisible calm, allusive
as the moon's shadow,
begets a hole deep as blindness seeking an eternal point
to expand into an infinite cloud
dark as night preceding existence.

Therein,
an opening.

My feral brain exploring silken avenues
and arbors drenched in lemon scent?

What nerve.

A fistful
of sweat emptying in nocturnal pathway's flickering dawn?

No chance.

Intrusive candor gelling immortal stillness
and mortal spasms

in texture
a baby can feel?

Mysterious
as the dance
with disembodied skulls,
a mask I can only observe.

1917, Amedeo Modigliani
Museum of Modern Art, New York

FOUNTAIN

White not orange,
cold not hot,
curved not square

hung on the wall,
put on the ground

holes for pipes,
holes for wee

a blessing to have
when you are full,
ignored
when you are not

an invention of a saint
or the necessity of the devil,
participation in the immortal Idea
or crunched to powder
when its usefulness expires

the damned could use it for hat,
a mouse for a nest

an artist for a prop.

1917,
(replica 1964) Marcel Duchamp
Tate Modern, London

SYPHON, GLASS AND NEWSPAPER

Vision has fractured, the way is broken,
carnal impetus shattered

the structure in balance.

The pieces convey total cessation
of influence—

the paper unreadable, the syphon inert,
the glass barely locatable.

Nihilating distance, negating time separating objects,
arriving at constant, direct sense,
superimposing dark lines
on the immediacy of matter.

Each time each instant is calculated
and rendered totally without passion,
reaching painstaking seriousness,
intense precision, the void beyond time.

With care, carving out knife edged perfect incisions
upon the Gorgon's engraving

headless.

1917, Juan Gris
Ludwig Museum, Cologne, Germany

METAPHYSICAL MUSES (MASKS)

Drink the spring
with lacerated tongue,
examine black ink with black eyes,
listen to steps on the moon
with numb eardrums

water tastes of blood,
the abyss reaches ocular nerves,
a seeker traipses on the outskirts
of sanity
with a bell around his neck.

Salty sweet liquid
in a chalice clogs the airways
when a simple man lifts it to his lips,
a tinkle sounds of laughter
the Savior heard
when the populace denied his coming,
the nescient wall between literature
and author reaches a depth untraversable

lift the mask
and the figment
we have known since childhood
will swirl in our spine,
unclasp the iron shield covering a heart
and a temporal pulse will beat on a chest

in transcendent allure,
unbutton the cloth that swathes our brain
and a face
in a mirror
will swim into view.

1918, Giorgio de Chirico
(Fondazione Cerruti)
Tokyo Metropolitan Art Museum, Tokyo

M'AMENEZ-Y

Barrage with a false associates
of play far castor language paint
on a inscription one portrait refined
the fine unto hypocrisy
less used
art transforming binder
with at
another
of inscription delivers the art
puns this crocodile
linseed painting
oil
the crocodile with foul smelling substance
of
connects the oil
oil
artist's in the teeth
the work reads studio
artist castor tears a top oil of

1919–20 Francis Picabia
(Dada Chance Poem)
Museum of Modern Art, New York

AROUND A POINT

Should I expand beyond a dying sun
and wet my brow
with rose blooming in aether,
or contract into the still voice
at the center:

lemon juice puckering my lips,
earth worms chewing on blood,
centipedes glowing green,
toadstools growing on stumps

to the sweet infant's empty crib,
and lie and dream:

snakeskin shed
and pink skin,
uvular quiescence and robes of white,
limpid sentinel and age-old light

to dull sounding harps and blighted tones,
a mortuary before the toll
and supplication
from a frog on death row:

pop me
and suffocate,
clog my ears with silt

in alliance
with an angel shedding feathers on my brain
and ardor ingrained in a fertile seed,
breathe again in a womb.

1920–25, Frantisek Kupka
Musée d art Moderne, Paris

STILL LIFE

Who can drink from color,
extract a perfect droplet from a scrawl,
derive nourishment from ever increasing momentum,
imbibe life's fulfilment
from texture saturated in trance?

A circle pursues never ending flawlessness,
a square the unalterable certainty
we subsist equally within its angles

a bottle, shaped to complement aesthetics
and function,
adumbrates reality,
our bodies fashion an allusive future

in the apotheosis from chaos
to order,
erect an epitaph:

"Our feet
were placed exactly
where they were meant to be."

1920–21, Amédée Ozenfant
National Gallery of Victoria, Melbourne

COMEDY

We drank blood.
We sucked pig's juice.
We imbibed venal fluid.
Please forgive us.
We are so stupid.
Shut up!
Damn you for drying me out,
hopeless crowd,
gluttonous lot.
Oh, I am frustrated
with your stupidity
and your needs.
I am sorry.
You are not to blame,
are you?

1921, Paul Klee
Tate Gallery, Liverpool, England

MAN IN A GREEN COAT

If I crack, green will drench my apparel,
orange-white smear the window looking on a garden

bulbs decay in the pulp between my ears,
stems wilt though my feet,
windswept leaves congeal under my fingernail.

If I burst
like a rotten gourd,
foetid air will rinse my hair,
brown polish my shoes aiming to scale Jacob's ladder.

When eye socket drip wet fire
and angels decry my ascent,
in the immanence
of a fall vested in the color
of Sheol,
I'll hold my head
in hands that slip from the bottom rung.

1921, Chaim Soutine
Museum of Modern Art, New York

NUDE WITH DRAPERY

I shan't evoke Daphne, Venus,
Chloe,
or a sylph stranded on the moon,
but she as she is,
naked and vulnerable
as scallop flesh under the gaze
of a predator.

I'll dispense with sylvan essence, aphrodisia
and frankincense stirred by golden fingers,
but bring forth the aroma
of pure soap and a natural wave

I have no time for querulous suitors,
emerald rainbows and queens redolent
with sweat

but, in an intimate,
once in a day routine,
the body of one
who, disposed to pink skin
and white cuticles,
will look into a mirror
and exclaim:

"There are no great heights for me to pursue,
no goals taking me away
from the hard work I must endure

but,
refreshed from an early morning bath,
I can step into a world I know
will receive me
with a polite,
"How do you do?
And,
Can I help you?"

1921, Suzanne Valadon
National Gallery of Victoria, Melbourne

VERNNONET

I have stood for many moments watching you, my love

for your eyes evinced the blue of a perfect day,
your skin the softness of a cloud
and your apparel,
worn with the insouciance of wind lifting the leaves,
the vital flecks of nature's hues
merging,
and becoming more vivid
as they separated from the background.

I drifted out of calm
and somnolence
in the face of burgeoning growth,
temptress of my shallow gifts,
and waited for her glance
from shimmering waves and open buds

for you evoke the tender vison I have had of love,
lost passion
and a heart broken.

1922, Pierre Bonnard
Aberdeen Art Gallery, Scotland

COMPOSITION WITH BLUE, RED, YELLOW AND BLACK

A clear sky after rain,
a daffodil, blood,
clouds,
and the abodes we build to surround loneliness

cowardice, danger,
despair,
melancholy,
and the quietude found in contemplation of nothingness

the idea, subliminal as no known name,
we can evince a doorway through a blaze,
structure steps
to reach outside pain,
efface torment,
subsist over shimmering gore below,
settle
in boundless blue

finally, surpass embodiment
in Nature
and the rhythms
of war.

1922, Piet Mondrian
Louvre, Abu Dhabi

THE REPRESENTATION OF HUMANITY

The forces above are calling
in a convoluted singing
to relieve myself of responsibility,
to embrace paradise,
ascend into Heaven without thinking.

The forces below
are pulling without caring for decency,
light, or security,
to Babelic undertones.
They beg to damn pain,
fight to darken all being,
blister to decay the good,
linger to attenuate healing.

The spiritual master is guiding me
to follow the Word posited in revelation

open to the subtle variations
of insight into the cosmos,
elucidate the path forward,
actively enquire with my own free thought
the mysteries of humanity.

The devil's henchman
is clasping my ankles,
pulling me into his maw,

gorging my faculties
with black odor,
tempting me to abide with cruelty.

I am not going to go now.
I will hold between bright, ineluctable light
and immersion in the abyss below.
My fortitude will be service,
my motivation love

firmly balanced between opposing desires,
my resolution

apotheosis.

1923, Rudolf Steiner
Goetheanum, Dornach, Switzerland

PIETA OR REVOLUTION BY NIGHT

You'll hold me, Papa, and rinse me
with tears

I know you'd like me cleaner than the moon.

You'll carry me
light
as a raindrop

prefer me fresh as morning dew.

Like a cut out child made of tissue,
you'll transport me to the outskirts
of indelibility

have me remain transparent as a whisper:

"I have no cause
to give you grief."

But, please, Papa,
fill me
with blood,
craft my feet with lead,
paint my eyes black

throw me to the floor.

1923, Max Ernst
Tate Gallery, London

THE MANDRILL

The void transfers a hole
into conscience,

glands secrete wild perfume,
shadows catch a hint of speed

out of your monkey skin

jump!

Soft footfall lands on a thorn,
pink flesh flares into noon,
tongues drip,
spiders retreat into gossamer

the black moon wet in a squall,
scars across your throat,
red points in your eye,
blood stains on a tooth

the day cringes from midnight.

1926, Oskar Kokoschka
Museum Boijmans Van Beuningen, Rotterdam

BOATS AND CLIFFS

Floating to and fro

forward, back, tossing, awash

embryonic shells open and close,
evince the white pearl torn out
and replaced with grit
to make more of the same.

Immersing fully
and quietly

core, heart, signifying, word

the seer,
who delves under the prow,
protects numinous parlance,
descries no precedent and faces the signs
out of nowhere.

Pointing to and fro

buoyant, head up, lapping, afresh

flotsam and debris sweep
in steady movement
like waves adrift a mooring.

1927, Paul Klee
Museum of Modern Art, Vienna

OCTOBER MORNING

I could pass you in the night and you wouldn't raise a glance,
catch your shadow
at noon,
hard edged as steel,
and you'd etch the darkness

through the day's long bite
of sunlight reflecting from a timepiece
till it burnt your forehead,
traverse my path warily
and attempt to avoid the glitter in my eyes

but in the absence
of coal, shunt and glint,
on the same plane
drenched in angelic sweat,
say hello

as strangers.

1927, Clarice Beckett
Art Gallery of South Australia, Adelaide

THE CURVE OF THE BRIDGE

For what purpose
would one want to stand
looking up at steel
and abandoning one's senses
to the rigor of stone and angularity?
Surely one's time
would be better spent
in the fields
where wildflowers grow,
imbuing an orgy of loveliness
with mist and color.

Yet,
here we are presented
with strict form
that does nothing to enliven the senses
with delicacy,
tender affection,
breathing, charming like.

Preposterous you may declare,
but for one instance in a solitary life,
it is possible
to witness unto the strength
of the few
who have dedicated their flesh
and sweat

to sweeping from the groves
where wattles flourish
unto the abode I rest in,
and imagine crossing the stretch separating me
from the profusion.

1928–29, Grace Cossington Smith
Art Gallery of New South Wales, Sydney

CIRCULAR FORMS

Embodiment—the cruel fate we must endure:
ice splinters in eyes,
gargantuan bones crushing anvils,
fish gums emulating lips

deliverance—
the freedom we conjure from our dreams:
untrammeled expansion from an inert center,
ever increasing from the last perimeter—
the full extent
of reaching beyond limitation,
the outward manifestation
of an exterior journey meeting the invariance
of hues at the zenith
and the hues of invariance at the nadir,
and between them
on a descending and ascending arc
the fountain of an eternal spring
and colors melting in silence

beyond the boundary of nescience,
the opposite blazing with light

the circle with an end,
darkness no beginning.

1930, Robert Delaunay
The Guggenheim Museum, New York

THE PERSISTENCE OF MEMORY

I could break open your jaw
and scatter teeth on the moon,
cut your nose with a butter knife
and piece by piece
construct an edifice to worship

you'll stand there entranced,
and think that time,
steady
as a mechanism built of steel and glass,
would melt like cheese
on a hot day.

In arabesques stolen
from an ancient script,
I'll dot the plains
as if ants knew the source
of the intimate Word

in squelches
of glue,
paste and earth,
I'll rebuild the dome above Jerusalem,
and call it my adobe flickering with angelic dust

you'll sit there, wondering,
and think I've embellished the landscape

with promise of timelessness
and unsequestered destinies foregoing pain.

From the scission in a fertile brain,
I'll extract needles
and firelight

in the temple under my navel,
I'll bring forth tulips
and raindrops

from the cavern under my feet,
I'll lift ghosts and succubi
into the dance between your eyes

you'll see them
as flaccid clocks,
and feign pleasure
at their burrowing into your blood.

1931, Salvador Dali
Museum of Modern Art. New York

TOWERS OVER CITY HALL

I am trapped in a jewel
and see no other
than facets twisted toward my desire
to escape.

To where?

Another plane contrarily structured to my abode—
luminous
yet dark,
colourful yet bland,
translucent yet obscure

the central point within
vertiginous
as an eye suspended on a cupola,
open to chance
as a groat flipped in a well,
exciting as a dot
of ink on fire.

You are a diamond
and will last longer than the disorder
you crave.

1931, Lyonel Feininger
Museum Ludwig, Cologne, Germany

VOICE OF SPACE

Drop in for a visit
and leave your calling cards:

I, for one, have nothing new
to divulge:

the world will still fire a plume
on a martyr's skull,
the goose fly to meet a wind
sending it backwards,
descent occur when ascent reaches the rain.

Unlike that, I have a more positive outlook:

breasts will seep rich red milk
until you have your fill

you won't burst and empty your innards

bloated, though, you'll still crave more.

Unlike them,
I'll transcend that rubbish
and pearlescent beyond the cravings
of the frenzied,
aver figments of fertility
will drip into a womb,

gestate
and rebirth as a cosmic queen:

a diadem above my brow,
a brooch on my spine,
sparklers on my teeth,
I'll twist you in my spindle

until threadlike bare
you'll encircle the moon.

1931, René Magritte
Guggenheim Museum, New York

AD PARNASSUM

Break into my heart
and you'll stand before my altar
like a child with blinkers.

Focus on my intent

bottomless the drift,
edgeless the whirl,
begotten the bedrock

the sun your eye,
the moon the glow in your brain,
the shadows
the entirety of your body.

Swim in underground rivers
until darkness absorbs your sight,
countenance the black flame
until the heat singes your feet,
be secretive unto the forgotten beforehand
until quietude envelops your descent

a blink
could awaken you
on a pinnacle.

1932, Paul Klee
Kunstmuseum, Berne, Switzerland

DINING ROOM ON THE GARDEN

Plant violets in my brain,
smear petal juice on the sun,
drench my veins with honey,
lathe skirting boards
with the stuff that flows from a goddess's breast

lachrymose slumber condenses like butter
on a wooden slab, an implosion
in an oracle sucks in detritus
and leaves vestiges of an earth baked
in somnolence.

Twist gild in my knuckles
stamp my signature on the floral plane,
lash my breath with burnished crème,
leave droplets in the space
guests will fill

foliage stains the entrance
to an eternal arbour,
clandestine sylphs enamored with the glint
in an iris
take up residence therein
and look at me
as if I eschewed the clamoring world

with wings of fire,
brush a pirouetting god

disentangle the tired bloom.

1934–35, Pierre Bonnard
Guggenheim Museum, New York City

HIROSAKI CASTLE

Loneliness countered
by insects swarming to the locus
receptive as a goddess's open heart,
frailty emboldened by straight lines
keen as a god's plunge
into rock,
sorrow supplanted with a bough of pink

charisma of Spring
a dance from ancient epochs settling in each scratch
of my hand.

Laziness defeated
by another bud opening with the verve
of a hidden source,
cluelessness made clearer
with the scent
that lasts only long
as the petal evades a brown tinge,
oblivion annihilated
by the eternal emptiness prefiguring each stalk,
window
and unerring curve in the eaves

castle and cherry mingling in one.

1935, Yoshida Hiroshi
Art Gallery of New South Wales, Sydney

YELLOW MIDDLE

Certitude—

that each element divorced from the center,
notwithstanding its impetus
to expand independently into a free-standing entity
capable of existing eternally
will, indeed,
effect a space where evolution is nihilation,
the mirror of creation absence,
the source of germination diminution.

Indubitability—

any object that suspends its relationship
with the other,
and expects to persist, ad Infinium,
in the glow of its own internal emanation
will, when the distance reaches its apogee,
find no support
for its edges collapsing into its outward thrust.

Definitude—

any speck, no matter how glorious,
will lose any semblance of the power
that keeps it beauteous as Beauty's Ideal
if, for a moment of self-adulation,

it transcends perfect harmony
in the eye of the Observer,

1936, Wassily Kandinsky
Museum Boijmans Van Beuningen, Rotterdam, Netherlands

CROWN OF BUDS II

Coeval with the sparrow
that lights on a nest to feed her young,
intimate as a father touching a son's lip
at the instant of birth,
candid as the heart that plunges into the well
to find a mate,
I'll swell with the chimes at midnight

fragmented as a jewel reflecting a connoisseur's eye,
disjointed as a child
in want of sound limbs,
irregular as a dancer losing the beat
in a tango,
I'll lift nothingness where it belongs—
distant from the edge

prescient as a ghost supplanting pallor
with density,
prophetic as a nun glimpsing the second coming
between her fingers,
erudite as a scholar acknowledging the gift
of understanding
far surpasses his centre,
in the morning before dew congeals

and the rays beat down upon the sward,
I'll open.

1936, Hans Arp
National Gallery of Victoria, Melbourne

WEEPING WOMAN

You could drink my eye bulging with an ocean,
she stop my bleeding with gauze,
he affix his lips
to my wet mouth,
a little one wash in the blubbering
that pours from my breast,
an angel suspended over my nose
twist it to face a pink bloom

they'll creep by without looking sideways.

A devil stokes a fire in my gullet,
the moon brightens a patch under my hair,
a messenger arriving from Samarkand proffers a gift
from a forbidden idol:

"If you flounder in my heat,
touch my toes with purple tongue,
and eat my brain,
you'll see the travesty
as a play
of chance on a rotting stage."

1937, Pablo Picasso
National Gallery of Victoria, Melbourne

DEATH AND FIRE

I'll dictate through membrane
transparent as melting glass
the reasons for my visit.

Eye gel will suffer
red fire in a cloud, brains dissolve
on a pyre,
hubris form white sockets I can fit perfectly within.

I can see you sweating,
choking on your bloated tongue.
You haven't much time left.

I can hear your genitals swell,
the moon stuff eye yolk in your pores.
The light will diminish.

Bulbs exude the perfume of bleeding glands,
bubbles pop
on foetid skin.
Watch me fade.

Catapults fling titbits into the mouth
of a saint,
ash configures the shape of an everlasting gnome,

belfries ring out the toll a demon hews on lime.
Pray before I go.

1940, Paul Klee
Kunstmuseum, Berne, Switzerland

GOOD HOPE ROAD

Eventually,
the moon will brush my lips,
a spider's web hang from ear
to ear,
the leave's green tinge my lids

in the bubble lifting from the spring,
I'll surrender to the colors
translucent on the orb,
and exclaim.

Paradise awaits a voyager—
the warm verge a place to rest.

Utopia sings of gallants
in ardor,
blossoms fine as transparent skin,
mosaics pieced together with red,
yellow
and blue.

The gravel road disappears into the hills—
a delightful place to tread.

Idyll strums a lyre
from the picturesque tavern upon a cloud.

Mailboxes contain letters
of how happy we are
to live here.

1945, Ashile Gorky
Museum of Fine Arts, Boston, Massachusetts

FIRST-CLASS MARKSMAN

The glint on a buckle
three hundred yards off,
a stationary crow
on the branch above,
the damp patch between his eyes

without hesitation,
I'll level my barrel,
take aim
and drive a bullet through his skull
to the bark behind.

1946, Sidney Nolan
Art Gallery of New South Wales, Sydney

A MAN POINTING

On the edge of a chasm
whose circumference transcends my point of view,
I am poised between the horror
at the finality of my existence
and the abyss floating
under my will to be,
interred in darkness
without knowing the meaning
of my sojourn

scarlet veins crisscrossing the vagueness.

Quite reluctant to make a move?
Immobile. Frozen?

I will not submit. I am erect.

I will stand while molten figures drip
toward Hades,
bare my entire being to the throbbing cosmos

with clarity, point the way

1947, Alberto Giacometti
Tate Gallery, London

EIDOS

Seek not to disfigure me with disease,
bury me with fungus,
blind me with curdled milk.

I am a simple wish
who merely wants to grow.

Don't tempt me with acres
of verdant lilies,
generations expunging distorted veins,
or mountains glistening with ice.

I am only a lowly subject
who'll deliver a replica
in the selfsame form of my birth.

Cancel not my aspiration to persist,
endeavor not to bleed me
of my yolk,
counter the urge
to suspend me from a boom
and drop me till I crack

in the essence of light,
contour and hard rock,

I'll wait incumbent
while you pass in my shadow.

1947, Barbara Hepworth
National Gallery of Victoria, Melbourne

INTERIOR WITH EGYPTIAN CURTAIN

Prescient lute,
in the flux of motionlessness,
play into the sounds
of color becoming edible in my throat,
animate the vibrant black
between swirls
of white,
strum radiance glowing on fruit.

Conscient Muse,
rest the outer behind my brain,
leak the inner into leaves
and fronds,
drip juice in my spine

in the crease
of a curtain,
dark
as blind Jupiter seeking Neptune
as a mate,
find an eye discovering nescience

for the duration circling Betelgeuse
imprint silence on my fingertips:

for nothing, and for all time,
I will love you.

1948, Henri Matisse (The Phillips Collection, Washington DC)
Hayward Gallery, London

AUTUMN RHYTHM

As a star I would leave a brilliance so great
it would burn your eyes
and inflame your heart

the moon, a sheen
where a shadow could find solace

a tree, globes of sap sticky
and fragrant with mountain air

myself, a wilderness of line,
swirl
and unintended noise
that obliterates the preceding.

If I were a mythical being
I could leap from one era
to another
and you could cling firmly to my ears

a colossus straddling two worlds,
eat the sky and you, swallow my sweat

a demigod,
burnish each planet with a golden brush

and you, pretend you were fire

merely me, condense everything beforehand
in a mishmash of becoming
and no ending

and you, bewildered by the potency of potential,
in an instant of subliminal focus,
recreate what you could have been.

1950, Jackson Pollock
Museum of Modern Art, New York

VIR HEROICUS SUBLIMUS

Is it blood without a vein,
sunset
without a sun, a rose petal
without a rose

blood with no plasma,
a sunset
with no sky,
a rose petal with no fiber

blood washing the air,
a sunset escaping light,
a rose petal abnegating the flower

and through to the other side

blood
in a finger,
a sunset over a mountain

deep in a melting heart,
a rose transcendent to fading petals?

1950, Barnet Newman
Museum of Modern Art, New York

CHRIST OF ST JOHN OF THE CROSS

Buttressed by love,
sustained
by Heavenly wisdom,
ye chant orisons,
ye fools.

"Save us,
dear Christ.

Arrest us in your bosom, camouflage us
in your crucifix,
daub us in red soles."

Who wants pain.

"Arrest arrest.

Keep us eternally in your sacrifice."

Pain,pain.

Worship pain, hah!

1951, Salvador Dali
City Art Gallery, Glasgow, Scotland

ITALIAN SQUARE

The statue immobile
as ice carved by the Gorgon's handmaid,
the train silent
as smoke suspended in a vacuum,
shadows black
as slumber predisposed to never waking,
the square brilliant
as orange light
filtered through a web hanging across the sun.

What do they have in common?
What right
do they have to co-exist?
None.

Even if the gauze
is lifted from my eyelids,
the lucence made less static
by a twist from motionlessness,
they'll never come together,

and I'll stand aloof
mesmerised by contrariness.

1951, Giorgio de Chirico
Art Gallery of South Australia, Adelaide

THE BLUE PHANTOM

I have no veins
to protrude into your heart,
no lymph to splash on your lips,
no gore to spread on the floor

I'll merely drift through aether.

I'm devoid of a skull to crack,
a leg to hold a simpering child,
an arm to twist into a satanic claw

in blue light, I'll merely float until exhausted.

There is no breath issuing from the eternal rise
and fall,
no positive charge enlightening my eyes
to see you lit up like the sun,
no body to tantalise an opposite
into penetrating my forbidden depth

in an ocean of indigo becoming paler
as the hue turns inward,
I'll merely surrender my desire for embodiment

undulate over the landscape
until the next lucky voyeur
is able to perceive my nonexistence.

1951, Wols
Museum Ludwig, Cologne, Germany

THE INVISIBLES

Frame rivets in a socket,
constrain flight on a thread of steel,
distil air
in solid globules melding iron
and lead.

We grew intestines when light hardened,
shaped our brains in a forge

as mercury condensed on a pinpoint,
erected the condominiums
we'll inhabit
for an eon.

Manufacture screws that hold a skull plate
to a brain,
produce filings
that grind a mechanism to a halt,
fashion nuts
that bolt an erection
to the afterlife bolting its reflection
to our intrusion.

We taste the metal
in our bones,
subsist
between the spire penetrating grey space

and disappearing in aether,
assign polar opposites their due reward:

embodiment embodying the abyss,
nescience annihilating the thing
clear
as clarity informing lucidity,
flawlessness effacing the speck
in an eye.

1951, Yves Tanguy
Tate Modern, London

KERRHON

Arcs circling on a path
away from the revolution of other turning lines

a consistent, constant,
ever-increasing returning to the source
beyond our darker, primitive condition

a center,
whose point of view
is the orbiting beyond its own isolated point,
yet certain
imaginative forces
will hold the entire entity
in one body,
each related to the other
by centrifugal expansion

a zero-point gaining magnitude as the pace increases,
breaking the barrier between the square structure
and awareness
which has no boundary
or limitation

momentum
completely overturning stasis

abnegating cosmic entropy
before the decrease into nothingness.

1953, Victor Vasarely
Modern Art Museum, Brussels, Belgium

RED COCK AND BLUE SKY

My brain bleeds joy
equally as my heart secretes thoughts,
my heart drips milk
equally
as a breast squeezes out words

the cock could be blue
and the sky red,
an automobile float
on aether
while a cloud conveys a passenger through steel
and wax.

A plant oozes oil
equally as an engine emits juice,
black evinces the absence
of density
equally as white contains the absence of all light

numinous layers
could wait
in anticipation of secular intent,
unbelieving minions readily accept the influx
of otherworldly eminence.

An eye begins to hear the adulation
of forgotten deities, an ear see the machinations
of a world in pain

a sentient earth dweller could feel the ingress of immortal calm,
an immortal inside the constriction
it barely endures, absorb the agitation
of one
who turns an opposite upside down.

1953, Fernand Léger
The National Gallery of Western Art, Tokyo

COLLINS ST, 5 P.M.

Give me one excuse
and I'll scale the streetlight,
cross the wires
and climb down the enchanted tree
to a lake brimming with Orion's sweat.

If I had my way,
I'd caress the moon with eager fingers,
plant it in my garden
and watch the bud wither at noon.

Privileged
as a mortal,
I'll elope with Aphrodite
and kiss the air between us.

"This way,
please.
Don't stop
until you reach a red light.

Pause and go."

1955, John Brack
National Gallery of Victoria, Melbourne

THE JOSTLERS

Twist my arm
and I'll fall, kick my shin and I'll topple,
tug my ear and I'll end up upside down.

Snort blue air in my eyes
and I'll blame you for losing my balance,
curse me again and I'll rage with white teeth,
mark me
as a coward and I'll pull you
to the ground.

From before clots formed
in blood
and the struggle incensed ganglia,
a cell tore apart.

Until an abeyance
of momentum,
we'll always strive,
argue and compete

in the listless,
sun-baked air,
hot as sand in a furnace,
we'll grapple

for supremacy
and call it 'fun'.

1957, Jeffrey Smart
Art Gallery of South Australia, Adelaide

OPENING

Shadows open to light,
light opens to shadows

a heart opens to love,
love opens to a heart

kindness opens to a wound, a wound closes to kindness

a seam opens to let the sun in,
mends,
and leaves a seam

a mouth opens for nourishment,
nourishment opens for a mouth

a savior opens for the world's pain,
the world's pain opens for a savior

the center opens for the entirety,
the entirety encloses the centre

a womb opens for birth,
heals, and awaits the sun.

1961, Bridget Riley
National Gallery of Victoria, Melbourne

CAMPBELL SOUP CANS

The glint on the can
as you open it,
the fear you may cut your finger,
the heavenly smell
reminiscent of a farmyard.

One thing
I have discovered
in eating Campbell's soup
for the past twenty years:

they all,
more or less,
taste the same.

1962, Andy Warhol
Museum of Modern Art, New York

UNTITLED

Violet:
deep
as subterranean pressure melding worm skin
and the shades a pharaoh wore
on the night of his ascension
into the bloated sky
a god secreted blood in.

Red:
the usurer's eyedrops
as she plans to extract fluid
from cochineals
and fill bulging orbs
as repayments for debts.

Orange:
the quiescent solace I seek
now I remember the colors are mine
to reflect a cuneiform brain,
radiance to saturate the root of all evil
and the intensity betokening ardor
congealed in stupor and insanity

mine to float free from.

1962, Mark Rothko
Staatsgalerie, Stuttgart, Germany

MAIMONIDES

If I could be certain of one belief,
indubitable as the tear on a rabbi's cheek
at the death of a friend,
the drip from a pipe after rain,
the flow from a gutter during a storm,
then make it,
as sure as sunrise over a crowded city,
the beat of a drum in a festival,
the step
of a child
to greet his father returning from war,
a rose clinging to a wall,
that I rise to meet the Author
of all I can be sure of.

1964, Amadeo Olmos Ruiz
Plaza de Tiberiades, Cordova, Spain

MESSAGE FROM A FRIEND

Salutations
from outer hemispheres
to a denizen belonging to the shadowland,
spiritless passenger
on the craft across the universe,
beckoning you to discover meaning
at the center.

You were torn from a womb before you could see,
fraternized with dark
to reveal a throbbing heart,
trusted embryonic formation
in the consciousness
which suffers limitation.

I have arrived to embody primitive insight,
ending your brains encircling the spirit,
ending aggression and angst
if you could rise higher in cosmic stratospheres
above gray dross
and sun blinkered eyes:

archetypal ennoblement waits
in direct sustenance granted.

1964, Joan Miro
Tate Gallery, London

GIRL WITH HAIR RIBBON

I'll wait in the rain
until eye shadow runs down
and lips smudge the window.

The interior so remote, the light so muted.
Is he fondling her secret?

I'll cling to the sill until my knees bloat,
my feet drench,
my shoulders droop in the wet.

Could he deny me for a slattern,
pass over my charms for a taste of her scent?

The leaves whip up under my dress,
birds guzzle the downpour,
an eave bends in the weight.

I am still beautiful, you know.
My nail polish reflects the sun,
my conscience,
clear
as paddy water in spring,
climbs above the storm.

My allure will never fail,
my eyes will always be blue

through the miasma of lies
and deceit, my ribbon control every strand.

1965, Roy Lichtenstein
Museum of Contemporary Art, Tokyo

A BIGGER SPLASH

Pull out every red tooth,
claw and talon seeking a brain,
leave only a blue
that softens like a sylph milking Aryan eyes
on tropical sand.

Eject every hue saturating light
with a temper a dog feels
when a master fails to revive,
reflect a satyr's breath condensing in balm
a blithe spirit
could smear on a thigh.

Efface every remnant
of blood and pulse entering the air

in the instant, white
as the rush from an excited blond,
still the surge
on a steady plane

in a gift
from a frozen dream,
hold the splash

in a temporal lobe
for eternity.

1967, David Hockney
Tate Gallery, London

THE ANCESTRAL GUWARK

Heard beyond the moon,
black as the tones a daughter fears
on the death
of her mother,
the carnivorous delight in a splayed carcass.

Heard,
distant
as a gullet receiving the first drops
of the first rain,
the forlorn lapse between cracked earth
and a dark cloud sweltering at noon.

Heard,
harsh as wind scouring fallen wood,
the solitary night reminding a listener
that although the silence
will encroach from below the terrain,
an unimpeded throat
will persist
in light and haze.

1969, Narritjin Maymuru
National Gallery of Victoria, Melbourne

KHURASAN GATE VARIATION II

What has white
to do with colour,
unless it contains them all in its pallor?

What has the moon to do with death,
unless it lights the path over the threshold?

What has pattern to do with individuality,
unless one finds purpose
in the miasma
of concord?

What has structure to do with absence

unless,
in the fractures
and rifts on density,
one finds an immediate silence pondering demise
floating to the surface?

1970, Frank Stella
Art Gallery of New South Wales, Sydney

MAUSOLEUM OF MOHAMMED V

Death tastes
of ardor,
the tomb smells of fresh air,
moonlight glances on marble

the end restored in a beginning.

The flight to paradise leaves a wake,
the blue sky stains a tile,
clouds congeal in templates

the gateway drenched in rose.

Dare to express abundance,
fear not to extol a man,
recede not
into cowardice

carvings reflect the infinite,
patterns emulate eternal spheres

the internal space, pregnant
with repose,

ever ready
to receive the awe of an onlooker.

1971, Cong Vo Toan
Rabat, Morocco

DISTORTED CIRCLE WITHIN POLYGON II

I could aim
for the devil's eye under a surreal lampshade,
but who'd believe it?

I could surmise that God gave green ecstasy,
but who'd think that anyway?

In a millionth of an iota,
far surpassing the reckless drive from an abandoned bloom,
I could sup nectar on angelic wings,
but who would contemplate such folly?

For the squillionth time,
released into perpetual sainthood,
I could treasure an archaic idol in golden hands,
but who would be able to see this?

At the root,
then,
I'll merely colour infinity
in an irregular patch of paradise
called 'home'.

1972, Robert Mangold
Rhode Island School of Art and Design Gallery, Providence

MERLION

We'll drench the sea
with spray,
rise through the waves to the sun,
roar
with acclamation:

We'll carve our destiny
in rock and steel,
hold fast
in the swirling wind.

There are no obstacles we cannot climb,
no depths to which we'll succumb.

Small though we are,
great we may be,
we'll survive.

1972, Singapore

COLUMNADE

You could speak
with irreverence dismissing nonsensical alignment,
emphasize disillusionment:

marked on a skull,
Eternity severs her leash
and behaves like a criminal
who whips children
into submission

encrusted with savagery,
the Archangel deceives us
and mutilates perfection

but embrace it,
because it doesn't mean anything

accept it
for what it is:

a simple shape made out of concrete,
a nice pattern arranged for the sake
of difference.

1973, Eduardo Ramirez Villamizar
Tryon Park, Manhattan, New York City

SOLSTICE

If the sun were grief,
we'd be saturated
with tears

the night joy,
blanketed with gifts
of brilliance

we'd look forward to long,
dark hours
and dread the zenith burning overhead

as the rich, red sunset lingered into twilight,
hope the brief interval before dawn
when trees
vaguely green stand like sentinels,
would deepen into velvet black,
and the light
so bright, focused and intense,
seeming to last an eternity,
surrender unto an interior
where dreams filter the glare,
illuminate kind eyes

transfigure imaginary voyages encountering a glow
Chronos would find hard
to ignore.

1974, Lesley Dumbrell
Art Gallery of New South Wales, Sydney

STUDY FOR SELF PORTRAIT

Extirpate the scent from my buttocks,
clean my eye socket of tears,
smear the cobwebs on my feet.
I'll flower like a daisy reaching the rays
of an unknown sun.
Brush profane utterance from my lips,
conceal my balls with a pure white orb,
twist my spine
from obscene surrender.

On the wings of Pegasus,
I'll fly to the pure land.

Unravel my veins until they're straight,
comb my hair until it curls,
twist my muscles
until smooth as Donatello's marble

Forsaking the death rattle,
I may,
if contorted out of my skin,
reach a reflection that doesn't horrify me.

1976, Francis Bacon
Art Gallery of New South Wales, Sydney

DOVE

Despite our tendency
to lapse into personal desire for things
other than given,
allow us to seek the words
you require at the instant you design,
free us to move where you lead,
gently challenge us
to address issues
relevant to our being here

immanent
in fresh blood and the pulse
of a heart,
instil the wisdom to realize you care
for our journey,
remind us to be constantly aware
you surround with life giving peace,
enable us to discern your texture
in the pattern of worldly affairs

through moments in faith,
simply reveal

we are capable of receiving visitation
from your Holy Self.

1979, Éric de Saussure
(Stained Glass) Church of Reconciliation, Taizé, France

CHANGES AND DISAPPEARANCES

To experience altitude between the poles
of anguish
and death,
a line portrays directionless instance, music
without sound,
pointedlessness
in aimlessness

vestiges of cruelty cut,
a moment sliced,
inroads
of passion cancelled

between insight and objective matter,
a surface realization harmonizes darker limitation
with enlightened knowing,
a variation in momentum

extant instance outside of confined space

1979, John Cage
City Art Gallery, Auckland, New Zealand

HE CAME BRINGING TALLOW

The Muse could from vertiginous heights
meld into flesh,
the lumbering gait
so disposed to self service
transform into a graceful step,
leave an imprint light as sunlight

the divine, enamored with gaiety
descend into tissue,
join the layers separating skin from blood

sedentary curves,
prolonging the cruel waste
of potential,
balance on one leg,
the dumfounded revoke chaos,
the irresolute resolve at the ocean's edge

illumined conscience,
undiscovered in realms bound by hard bone,
undetected in furrows
and banks of grey matter,
congeal in fat

a fracture,
aware of the shift
from increase to decay,

solid to fluid,
the plenum to the abyss,
concretize
in an upright stance

intimate guidance transcend four corners.

1983, Joseph Beuys
Museum Kunstpalast, Düsseldorf, Germany

MOTHER AND CHILD

I know of no hymn,
no prayer, no speech
that adequately expresses a mother's warmth.

I have tasted no delicacy,
no fruit,
no meal that can supply the richness
of a mother's nourishment.

I have felt no heavenly aura,
no otherworldly encirclement,
no ineffable power that manifested the essence
of a mother's protection.

and finally,
I have seen no work
of art, no chiselled marble,
no form representing the love
I felt
as an infant that brings into focus
the tenderness of a mother's bond.

1983, Henry Moore
St Paul's Cathedral, London

MOUNTAINS

Valleys are inverted mountains,
mountains are valleys upside down.

Clouds taste of black soil,
light saturates the deepest well.
Could there be a clue
to the revolution?

The cosmic settles in dust,
the arboreal climbs to Saturn.
How to express the infinite
in a grain,
the kernel outside the parameters
of sight?

Eventide suppresses darkness
in the glint of dying day,
midnight annihilates noon
in the instant of a chime.
How to preserve both in a heartbeat?

1985, Miriam Cahn
Tate Gallery, London

SUSPENDED STONE CIRCLE II

If a voice had a shadow,
it would flicker
and dance like vague wisps on an ethereal carpet

a heart, divulge a blind chasm,
which must be crossed
to reach purer blood
in a never-ending stream

the earth,
a black moon
where the hare
of Chinese myth shivers endlessly

under a consistent light source,
rock
suspended from a roof,
a pattern far removed
from the inertia under their brethren
embedded in soil

the eyes of a viewer,
a fluttering orb chancing a place

to rest

in the unmoving shadowland on the floor.

1988, Ken Unsworth
Art Gallery of New South Wales, Sydney

THE DANCE

As night bled into veins
and enhanced a daydreaming pulse,
a bruise on a knee blanched,
a curl on a child's forehead lifted,
and couples sought
to remember the initial warmth
they felt as courting lovers

a silvery glow persuading their deeper longing
to emulate the pause,
starts, flashes, and twirls
of the elemental force driving toward redemption

heartbeat, lilt, perspiration, brow

quizzicality, amour, forcefulness, thought:

I can hear you compelling me
to join you once more
before the night ends,
before elocution mimicking interstellar motion resounds:

Return to your beds
and freeze

insouciance will partake inevitably in its opposite,
and be quelled

slumber negate awareness

twilight transform
into shadows etched on finality.

1988, Paula Rego
Tate Gallery, London

TWO LAKES IN VIRGIN FOREST

I don't belong
where stars asterisk the night
with premonition of turmoil,
nor subsist
in heightened conscience transiting from melancholia
to paradise

a dying sun beyond terrestrial vision,
climes forewarning the strictures of Saturn

mine is the silence of a moonlit lake,
the barren outcrop flecked with snow,
an insect forced to surrender to loneliness

my abode isn't the bright lights
and glitter of cosmopolitan life,
nor transforming daubs
suffered in black ink

in the sigh of an ancient pine,
a trunk devoid of vigor,
I find a home fragile
as the candor under my heart,
dark as the mood in my breast.

1988, Kyuichiro Aihara
Kawagoe City Art Museum, Kawagoe, Japan

LOOK AT AN APPLE
DIGEST AN IMAGE
A SELF-PORTRAIT

Having no end
to the distance encircling suffering,
the extent
of neurosis,
the outreach of insanity,
will the Word be forthcoming?

Disappearing to the extreme limit
of indistinguishability on unsightedness,
negation on absence,
and motionlessness
on an expanding zero,
will the unanswerable be questioned?

Inhuming the Resurrection,
blinding the conscience and spirit,
will the frontal lobe expand into uninhabited regions
aware
and conscious of nothingness?

1989–91, Remy Zaugg
Museum of Modern Art, Frankfurt, Germany

GODDESS

Your finger could brush the web from my eyes,
your tongue lick the tears
from my lids,
your mouth suck the black spot
from my gel

then I could see you as your really are—

a radiant flush pristine as dawn.

Your heart could beat faster
into mine,
your neck elongate the bid
of my larynx to reach over clouds,
your spine stick to my bones,
enabling me to stand upright

then I could withstand the gale,
the tempest,
the freezing winds as you do—

a flame annihilating purblind ghosts
on the prowl.

Your abdomen could enclose mine in rapture,
your throat bleed into each word I utter,
your wrist bend

with each dot,
stroke and daub of my hand

then,
with minstrels acclaiming the substance
of the ethereal becoming concrete,
you could manifest
on a stretch of white under candlelight—

a real presence who moves amongst us.

1992, Jangarh Singh Shyam
Art Gallery of New South Wales, Sydney

IRON: MAN

Eyes of lead, lungs
of black dust,
heart
of gold melt in the cauldron

fingers like rivets,
bones
like scaffolding,
a spine
like a nail arise in a new mold
that begets the spirit of industry

teeth of zinc,
brain of steel,
cross
of metal stare into the squares you have erected

shoulders in a vise,
hips of stone,
feet punched in a plate,
bind with the concrete
you have constructed.

1993, Antony Gormley
Victoria Square, Birmingham, England

UNTITLED FROM FLIGHT FANTASY SERIES

I'll affix my body to a plaque
and embellish it with hair, droppings
and the scat of a scarecrow.

You'll rise
and applaud

"Beauty
is in the eye of the beholder."

I'll drain faeces from my fingers
and smear it in a gallery.

No one will know the difference,
and call it a masterpiece.

Art belongs in alleys,
the sewer
and tenements where rats breed
and die.

You'll acclaim the brilliance
and preserve the squalor for posterity.

Wallpaper bleeds readymade paint,
a flower drips ointment meant to cure sores.

You'll clap
and exclaim
we've reached the high point
of evolution.

1995, David Hammons
Tate Modern, London

MAMAM

Even when darkness shrouds an incumbent
upon a black rock,
mother's warmth will encompass the earth

a forlorn creature rises from the abyss,
mother's salve will heal its wounds

an infirm ghost
has lost the pillar enabling it to float
into vision,
mother will fill it
with her milk

presentiment envisages the other side
of death,
mother will still encounter dearth
of gravity
with light

the martyr begs to have his reward
beyond the spike through his brain,
mother will rain tears on the scars

a blind addict craves light
to know where to crawl,
and expects a wall to obstruct his search

mother,
laden with eggs
and thoroughly concerned
to find a nest
to nurture her own,
with the strength of a thousand warriors,
will still find time
to lift the barrier obscuring the path
to a well washing an eye.

1997, Louise Bourgeois
Art Gallery of New South Wales, Sydney

WANJINA

Moisture in an eye,
blood in a vein, fluid from a sore

one white cloud, sunset's demise,
white water rushing down a hill

raindrops pattering on bark,
saturated clumps of bush,
wet fur
and overflowing creeks

sweat
after a hunt,
swimming in a deep pool, matted hair
and trickling down a spine

a profusion
of wildflowers after a drought,
the long cool slaking of thirst,
joyful floundering in an acre of mud

the black
and blue build up day after day

in an instant, to an expectant gathering,
the breaking open to the plains below

the bubbles,
gurgles,
and sighs of an infant foreshadowing words
an adult utters
before they wither away.

1998, Lily Karadada
National Gallery of Victoria, Melbourne

21st Century

BABEL

With the ubiquity of our clamor,
God's response
would be drowned out

the din of our aspiration,
God's word suffocated

the noise of our ascent,
God's transcendent peace,
the focus of a dying recluse,
damned in cacophony.

2001, Cildo Meireles
Tate Modern, London

FLOWER THROWER

My temper will explode in petals

blossoms exude fragrance, bile,
wrath
and incalculable rage against disenfranchisement

shower the deranged
with color, softness,
and plucked early on a frosty morning,
heads dissolving on the ground
in Spring

clouds imminent
as nature unfolding in receptivity,
eye with iris,
lips with dew

bouquets in a brain.

2002, Banksy
Banksy Exhibition, Sydney Town Hall, New South Wales

THE SPIRE

The past will no longer encroach
upon sensibility,
hardship
and starvation no longer impinge
upon a truly liberated conscious aspiration,
nationality
no longer provide a framework
to celebrate achievement.
We'll penetrate the skies with a stainless capacity
to penetrate the skies
with a stainless resolve to penetrate the skies
with a stainless erudition
mirrored
in stainless evocation
of a point penetrating the skies.

2002, Ian Ritchie (Architect)
Dublin, Ireland

UNTITLED (BACCHUS)

Extravagant night,
let me dwell in your skull,
enact the contours of your brain,
the curves of your lobes,
the swirl
of your veins

then,
when an observer
is confused by intention,
I can readily say,
"It wasn't 'me,'
it was 'it'.

Vibrant 'it',
out on your own,
lost to an owner,
detached from purpose,
when an observer asks of you, "Why"?
you can respond:

"I have no idea."

2005, Cy Twombly
Tate Modern, London

UNTITLED (I-IX)

Released from criticism, doubt,
the echo of centuries imposing static principles
on the flow from primal depths,
volition manifests in rhythm preceding the Word's dictation
on volition.

Liberated from doctrine, idea,
the spurious demand of History
to make sense of the minutest instance
and,
in violation of the burst
of energy erupting in nomenclature,
meaning or linear structure
from then,
to now, to will be,
transcend the flux promulgated in determinacy.

Out of the trough subsuming movement
to thought,
I submit to nothing,
and I to no I,
and no I to everything.

2008, Cy Twombly
Louvre, Abu Dhabi

WIRINGPA

In the hole—water,
in the water—stillness,
in the stillness—light,
in the light—return

in the return—
a presence that has never gone,
in the presence that has never gone—silence,
in the silence—generation,
in the generation—a tree

in the tree—pith,
in the pith—water...

2009, Simon Hogan
Spinifex Country Exhibition
D'Lan Contemporary Gallery, Melbourne, Victoria

RISE

Your light is not the glow of a candle,
the flickering end
to a rainy day

brilliance
so intense
the waters of the Loch burnish.

Your luminance
is not artificial blue distorting figures
in a puddle

the eternal flame annihilating the shadow
which pours into my brain.

The center
isn't a spark hidden in ice
or smothered in smoke
and bad air

free from a pall
on bright eyes, the ascension,
not unlike the morning devoid of night's fatigue,
assuming prominence over rejuvenated growth.

2011, Wolfgang Buttress
Broadway Roundabout, Belfast, Northern Ireland

LITTLE GIRL WITH TEDDY

If I were teddy,
I'd be cuddled every night,
tucked in bed and read my favorite story.

Once upon a time,
when the wind howled
and the windows shook,
an angel appeared and said:

"My light will rest upon your soul,
rhymes
of Heaven float to your ears,
the tempest subside and wildflowers appear."

When I fell upon the floor,
I'd be picked up,
brushed off, my eyes polished,
and the little rip in my seam sewn together.

If the lights went out unexpectedly,
I'd be reached for,
patted,
and sung the little song we know so well:

Mummy
and daddy are asleep,
ghosts lie under the bed,

strangers tap the door,
but I'll stay with you,
warm your feet, tickle your hand

make sure
you know
the lights will turn on again.

2012, Sam Philip
Holocaust Museum, Jerusalem, Israel

MISS SPRING

I can sparkle
with the energy of dawn,
gleam with frost on tender buds,
open with the sunlight
on my pores.

If you had a second,
you'd feel the breeze in your hair,
dew above your lips,
and flickering,
colorful as a butterfly's flight,
on an iris.

I can exude perfume
when the warm night meets an apogee,
refresh the moon lighting up my eyes,
surprise the woodland
in veils
of green and blue.

When the wheel turns to the solstice,
you may disperse dandelion fluff
with hot breath,
catch petals drifting to earth,
caress lamb's wool an hour or two
after birth.

I,
however,
despite my delicate smile
and ready for anything countenance,
wish I could enter your grasp

on the crest
of a tear
when the cherry blossoms were at their height,
break off a twig
and pin it to my breast.

2012, Yoshitomo Nara
Yokohama Museum of Art, Yokohama, Japan

REFLECTION MODEL (ITSUKUSHIMA)

On a black lake,
absence above reflects nothingness below,
a brilliant moon shines upon an inner pond,
and the stanchions supporting the roof
mirrors the selfsame structure beneath.

No visitants walk the corridors,
no vagrants sleep
in the lower rooms,

in the erection toward heaven
and the construction
toward hell meeting halfway,
only divine potential
bound in limits
erases clamor and friction

2013–14, Takahiro Iwasaki
National Gallery of Victoria, Melbourne

THE FUTURE

I heard they had space
long ago they could call their own,
at least a few square feet
where they could gaze
at their neighbors looking back at them

a structure on which to climb
and bars to hold,
and pretend they were strongmen
who could construct figments out of the ordinary:

a blister on the moon
with air that smelled of oil and grease,
a dirigible climbing into clouds
they could actually see,
a temple
where white clad incumbents invoked the transcendent spirit
said to divest humanity
of mortal fear.

Also,
Sometimes
when their mother wasn't watching,
they could hang
arms outstretched, legs dangling in midair,
to show courage

no matter their circumstances,
they could face danger
with renewed vigor
we lost centuries ago.

2014, Elmgreen & Dragset
Tel Aviv Museum of Art, Israel

BIT. FALL

If I were the sun,
I'd like to light up fish
that swam though a pebbled stream,
illuminate the Baptist pouring life
on the head of a child,
make clear the recesses hiding golden idols
from view

a waterfall,
splash
on every rock until it feels the freshness of an Arctic dawn,
plunge until I reach the limpid pool
hundreds of feet below,
gurgle and roar
till I numb the senses
of an illiterate churl

a word,
represent a thing
so an artist could purchase it from a catalog,
express the eternal essence of beauty,
ardor
and virtue
humanity aspires to
before I disappear in haste,
never to return,
convey the profound instance

unto anyone
who can read it as 'inconsequentiality.'

2016, Julius Popp
Museum of New and Modern Art, Hobart, Tasmania

VENUS

If I idolize her curves,
it will reflect
to my pale skin

contemplate her beautiful face,
her gaze meet mine
halfway

lust after her secret recesses
hidden under her shine,
moonlit blood reach my shadow

if the light source, intense
and steady,
cause me to blink,
I'll forget I adore her
and,
ecstatically,
wondrously, and out of my skin,
descry her love for me.

2016–20, Jeff Koons
National Gallery of Victoria, Melbourne

DIALOGUE

Hide
in red and gulp its quick

the leak from a sentinel's open vein,
heavenly sap sheening an iris,
pulmonary bubbles breaking on glass.

Saturate glands
with sunset hues

a lantern showing the way
to the center,
the slice
of an organ converting pimento into inner life,
divine ascension freeing a pulse
from incarceration.

Wash tears
from a bleeding eye

the seer who saw my demise.

2017, Lee Ufan
National Gallery of Victoria, Melbourne

TWO STEP

The breath on my cheek
is telling me that you love me.
Let's dance.

The voice
in my head
is telling me of patterns
I haven't forgotten.
Let's dance.

The urge in my spine
is telling me
I can spring.
Let's dance.

The combustible pressure
up
and down my legs is telling me I can forget fatigue.
Let's dance.

The sun
and moon swing like orbs
of delight
in front of my eyes.
We'll dance

and pulse
and dance some more.

2021, Nina Chanel Abney
Art Gallery Of New South Wales, Sydney

UNEARTHED LEAVES

Ground
in the heap,
moldering foliage retains the form
of primeval monsters devouring need
to rise from the layers assigned at birth

sentenced to a rotting substratum,
greedier creatures consume veins
and color preceding growth
a newborn feels
on breathing fresh air

saturated
in blood
and must,
crawling things take in the first stirrings
known to a shoot

disguised
as brittle patterns echoing demise,
lurking even deeper than a bundle
of roots,
a living force fears no decay,

corruption,
or threat of annihilation.

2024, Sandra Mujinga
Yokohama Museum of Art, Japan